17/99

D0099000

MYSTERIOUS
Realms

MYSTERIOUS
Realms

*Probing Paranormal,
Historical, and
Forensic Enigmas*

Joe Nickell with John F. Fischer

PROMETHEUS BOOKS • BUFFALO, NEW YORK

Published 1992 by Prometheus Books

Mysterious Realms: Probing Paranormal, Historical, and Forensic Enigmas. Copyright © 1992 by Joe Nickell with John F. Fischer. All rights reserved. No part of this publication may be reproduced, stored in a retrieval system, or transmitted in any form or by any means, electronic, mechanical, photocopying, recording, or otherwise, without prior written permission of the publisher, except in the case of brief quotations embodied in critical articles and reviews. Inquiries should be addressed to Prometheus Books, 59 John Glenn Drive, Buffalo, New York 14228-2197, 716-837-2475. FAX: 716-835-6901.

96 95 94 93   5 4 3 2

Library of Congress Cataloging-in-Publication Data

Nickell, Joe.
    Mysterious realms : probing paranormal, historical, and forensic enigmas / Joe Nickell with John F. Fischer.
        Includes bibliographical references.
        ISBN 0-87975-765-5
        1. Parapsychology—Case studies. 2. History—Miscellanea. 3. Forensic sciences—Miscellanea. 4. Curiosities and wonders. I. Fischer, John F. II. Title.
BF1029.N526   1992
001.9′4—dc20   92-36998
                                                                                              CIP

Printed in the United States of America on acid-free paper.

001.94
NIC
1992

In memory of our fathers:

J. Wendell Nickell (1914–1983)
Hans F. Fischer (1916–1983)

Contents

7

Acknowledgments

Once again we are grateful to Paul Kurtz, publisher of Prometheus Books, for allowing us to compile this casebook, and to the entire staff of Prometheus with whom it is always a pleasure to work.

In addition to those whose assistance is acknowledged in the respective chapters, we again express our appreciation to Lieutenant Drexel T. Neal, Lexington-Fayette Urban County Division of Police, Lexington, Kentucky, for special assistance; Robert H. van Outer, Lexington, for photographic work; the dedicated staffs of the Margaret I. King Library, University of Kentucky, and the John F. Kennedy Memorial Library, West Liberty, Kentucky, for their help over the years; the entire staff of the Committee for the Scientific Investigation of Claims of the Paranormal, including Barry Karr (executive director), Kendrick Frazier (editor of the committee's journal, the *Skeptical Inquirer*), and the members of the executive council; and Ella T. Nickell for typing our investigative reports and the manuscript for this book.

1

Introduction

Mysteries have always fascinated me. Some of my earliest memories are of being spellbound by the old radio crime dramas; later I clipped and saved the occasional Dick Tracy comic-strip feature, "Crimestopper's Textbook"; and eventually I discovered that master of deduction who resided at 221B Baker Street in Victorian London. A few years ago I was amused at recognizing how I had come full circle when philosopher Paul Kurtz described me to a reporter as "the modern Sherlock Holmes."[1]

Now I am able to present the third collection of my investigations. The first, *Secrets of the Supernatural* (Prometheus Books, 1988), was also written with John F. Fischer, my partner since 1978, and it focused on our investigations of "the World's Occult Mysteries"—for example, such "paranormal" enigmas as the "Riddle of the Crystal Skull," the "Specter of 'Spontaneous Human Combustion,'" and "Phantom Pictures: Self-Portraits of the Dead."[2]

My second casebook, *Ambrose Bierce Is Missing* (University Press of Kentucky, 1991), featured *historical* investigations: such cases as the identity of the Nazi war criminal known as "Ivan the Terrible," the authenticity of Abraham Lincoln's "Bixby letter," and other mysteries, including, of course, Bierce's disappearance.[3]

Now, in this volume we present a mixture of both "paranormal" and historical cases, together with a third type: forensic investigations. Actually many of the cases do not fit easily into a single category, but all partake of a certain quality of strangeness—such as might be associated, say, with a gothic novel or the tales of Edgar Allan Poe.

Secret codes and buried treasure, macabre relics, mysterious deaths, ghostly visitations, and other unexplained phenomena—such are the stuff that mysteries are made of. At least they are in this compendium of some of our most interesting and challenging cases:

- "The Gray Lady's Ghost" examines the spine-tingling phenomena that reportedly transpire in a historic house. The ghost has even been photographed, but is it truly a supernatural manifestation?

- "Assassin's Double" answers the question: "Did Lee Harvey Oswald really kill President Kennedy or—considering an attorney's startling evidence—was the assassination instead carried out by a Soviet look-alike?

- "The Legend of Beale's Treasure" studies the Beale Papers, which describe an early American bonanza. However, the treasure's location is protected by unsolved ciphers. Are the papers authentic or part of a grand hoax?

- "Eyeless Sight" investigates the possibility that some people are capable of "psychic" viewing. If they are not, as skeptics maintain, how do they perform such feats as driving a car while securely blindfolded?

- "The Crashed-Saucer Documents" assesses the authenticity of the "MJ-12" papers. If they are to be believed, crashed UFOs have actually been retrieved and—together with their embalmed humanoid pilots—are kept at a secret government facility. Is the story fact or fiction?

- "The Case of the Shrinking Bullet" analyzes the evidence in a death that first seemed a murder, then a bizarre suicide. What was the real solution to this seemingly insoluble forensic mystery?

- "The Piltdown Perpetrator" examines conflicting theories concerning who faked the notorious "missing link" skull. Can additional evidence settle the matter?

- "Miraculous Blood" investigates how—in apparent defiance of physical laws—the congealed blood of the martyred Saint Januarius periodically liquefies. Is this a modern miracle?

- "Surviving a Fiery Fate" relates the story of Jack Angel who suffered mysterious burns. But did he actually survive the legendary "hell's fire"—the alleged phenomenon of spontaneous human combustion?

- "The Crop-Circle Phenomenon" looks at the strange circular depressions and even more elaborate configurations that have been appearing annually in British fields of grain crops. Are they the result of "wind vortexes," or UFOs, or some other phenomenon?

As with our previous investigations, these represent serious attempts to get to the bottom of these mysteries, to discover the most likely explanation in each case. We decry alike an attitude that on the one hand is too credulous, too accepting of the fanciful, and that, on the other, is too closed-minded, that represents a dismissive, debunking stance. Those in either camp are similar in one respect: they have their minds made up, and—if they attempt to investigate at all—thus proceed in reverse order. They start with the desired or expected answer and work backward to the facts, instead of allowing the evidence to *lead* them to the probable conclusion.

An example of such a biased approach, as tragic as it is clear, is evident in the defense of the notorious Shroud of Turin, which is alleged to be the genuine cloth—among some forty vying for the honor—that wrapped the crucified body of Jesus. Whereas the preponderance of evidence—the cloth's lack of prior historical record, the reported forger's confession, the presence of paint pigments, and so on—clearly indicates the "shroud" is the handiwork of an artist, certain religious zealots have aggressively sought to prove otherwise. They offer one rationalization for the lack of provenance, another for the confession, still another for the pigments. And when the cloth was carbon dated by three laboratories, proving it was made about 1300, more rationalizations came: no doubt, they insisted, the tests were in error, or perhaps a burst of radiant energy at the moment of Christ's resurrection had altered the carbon ratio.[4]

The shroud investigations help demonstrate some of the rules that should be followed in such cases. First of all, it typically being difficult to prove a negative, the burden of proof must fall not on the skeptic but on whomever would make a particular claim. In addition, proof must be commensurate with the extent of the claim—hence the maxim, "Extraordinary claims require extraordinary proof." Another important principle is known as "Occam's razor" (after the fourteenth-century philosopher William of Occam), also called "the maxim of parsimony." It holds that the simplest tenable explanation—that is, the one involving the fewest assumptions—is most likely to be correct and thus is to be preferred.[5]

Among the logical fallacies to be avoided is the argument *ad ignorantiam,* literally, appealing "to ignorance." For example, when shroud proponents imply that the image on the cloth cannot be explained and therefore must be miraculous, they are making an *ad ignorantiam* argument. (They are also guilty of error or deliberate misrepresentation at the same time, since the "photographically negative" image is actually only quasi-negative, and similar quasi-negative images are easily produced by an artistic technique similar to gravestone rubbings.)[6]

Our insistence that mysteries should neither be fostered nor suppressed but rather should be *solved* reflects our investigative backgrounds. John Fischer is a forensic analyst with a Florida crime laboratory and an experienced crime-scene investigator whose work has earned him numerous law-enforcement commendations. He is also president of a corporation that specializes in forensic research, including microchemical analyses (e.g., identifying blood substances) and instrumental analyses (especially in the field of laser technology). His articles have appeared in such publications as *Law Enforcement Technology, The Journal of Forensic Identification,* and *Fire and Arson Investigator,* and he has given presentations to the International Association for Identification, the Federal Bureau of Investigation (FBI), and French law-enforcement agencies.

I myself am a former investigator with a world-famous detective agency who is now an investigative writer. In addition, I serve on the executive councils of both the Committee for the Scientific Investigation of Claims of the Paranormal and the Historical Confederation of Kentucky. In earlier years I also worked professionally as a stage magician (having been resident magician at the Houdini Magical Hall of Fame in Niagara Falls, Ontario), as well as a museologist and a newspaper "stringer." I also have a strong background in historic document examination and am author of *Pen, Ink, and Evidence: A Study of Writing and Writing Materials for the Penman, Collector, and Document Detective.*[7]

The diversity of cases presented here has not only tapped our varied areas of expertise—blood chemistry and other forensic fields, stage magic, document examination, and so on—but in addition it has required that we have the assistance of experts in such other fields as psychology, physics, linguistics, photography, computer science, forensic identification, pathology, even agronomy.

Now it is the reader's turn to join in. The following ten narratives permit the interested to look over our shoulders as we search for clues and sift the evidence in a variety of investigative adventures. But be forewarned: these are indeed "mysterious realms."

Notes

1. Quoted in Karen Brady, "Shroud Researcher Explains His Doubts to WNY Skeptics," *Buffalo News,* April 25, 1988.

2. Joe Nickell with John F. Fischer, *Secrets of the Supernatural: Investigating the World's Occult Mysteries* (Buffalo: Prometheus Books, 1988). Other cases in the book include "The Ghost at Mackenzie House," "Incredible Disappearances," "Synchronicity and the Two Will Wests," " 'Witching' for Hidden Gold," "Miraculous Image of Guadalupe," the "Bleeding Door," and "Restless Coffins: The Barbados Vault Mystery."

3. Joe Nickell, *Ambrose Bierce is Missing and Other Historical Mysteries* (Lexington, Ky.: University Press of Kentucky, 1992). Also treated are the mystery of the Nazca lines, John Swift's "lost" silver mines, spurious D. Boone artifacts, a "missing" colonial text, the source for Hawthorne's "Veiled Lady," and the Shroud of Turin.

4. See Joe Nickell, "Unshrouding a Mystery: Science, Pseudoscience, and the Cloth of Turin," *Skeptical Inquirer* 13, no. 3 (Spring 1989): 296–99. See also Joe Nickell, *Inquest on the Shroud of Turin,* 2d updated ed. (Buffalo, N.Y.: Prometheus Books, 1988).

5. For a fuller discussion see Robert A. Baker and Joe Nickell, *Missing Pieces* (Buffalo, N.Y.: Prometheus Books, 1992).

6. See Nickell, *Inquest,* 95–106.

7. Lexington, Ky.: University Press of Kentucky, 1990.

Select Bibliography

Altick, Richard D. *The Scholar Adventurers.* New York: Macmillan, 1951.
    Fascinating investigations of a literary and historical nature.
Binder, David A., and Paul Bergman. *Fact Investigation: From Hypothesis*

to Proof. St. Paul: West, 1984. Legally oriented text treating such matters as gathering and evaluating evidence, formulating hypotheses, developing proof, etc.

Frazier, Kendrick, ed. *Science Confronts the Paranormal.* Buffalo, N.Y.: Prometheus Books, 1986. Investigative articles and skeptical essays reprinted from the *Skeptical Inquirer* (the official journal of the Committee for the Scientific Investigation of Claims of the Paranormal).

O'Hara, Charles E. *Fundamentals of Criminal Investigation.* 3d ed. Springfield, Ill.: A standard text on investigative procedures and basics of forensic identification.

Schultz, Ted, ed. *The Fringes of Reason: A Whole Earth Catalog.* New York: Harmony Books, 1989. An attempt at a balanced treatment of various fringe subjects, described as "A Field Guide to New Age Frontiers, Unusual Beliefs & Eccentric Sciences."

Winks, Robin W., ed. *The Historian as Detective.* New York: Harper & Row, 1969. Excellent textbook on historical investigation, with essays on evidence, biographical research, lost texts, etc.; includes case studies on the Kennedy assassination, the Dead Sea Scrolls, and many others.

2

The Gray Lady's Ghost

The Legend

For over a century—if countless testimonials are to be believed—she has glided through the spacious corridors, trod noiselessly the antique stairway, and lingered in the chamber that has since become known as the "Ghost Room." Described as a small, trim woman, she is called the "Lady in Gray" or simply the "Gray Lady." Her address is 218 Wilkinson Street, Frankfort, Kentucky—a historic landmark known as Liberty Hall (see fig. 1), which previously hosted such guests as Lafayette, presidents Madison and Monroe, and Aaron Burr.[1] Since 1956 it has been maintained by the National Society of The Colonial Dames of America in the Commonwealth of Kentucky.

According to legend the lady is the earthbound spirit of an aunt of Margaretta (Mason) Brown (1772–1838) whose husband, John Brown (1757–1837), was one of Kentucky's first two senators. Brown built the Georgian mansion in 1796 as a home for his aging parents, naming

19

ALBUQUERQUE ACADEMY
LIBRARY

it Liberty Hall after the Virginia academy that his father had founded. He and Margaretta were married three years later, and in 1801 they moved into the brick home with their infant son, Mason. Another son, Orlando, was born in that year. The Browns' next two sons died in infancy, but in 1807 Margaretta gave birth to their last child, a daughter named Euphemia.[2]

Euphemia was a precocious child and her parents' delight, and when she became ill and died in 1814, John and Margaretta largely withdrew from social life and immersed themselves in religion. Indeed, Liberty Hall became known as "The Preacher's Hotel," due to the numerous ministers who were welcomed there.[3]

At this time, Margaretta's aunt, who was reportedly moving to Illinois from her home in New York, came to Kentucky to console her niece.[4] Sources give scant, conflicting details about her arrival and subsequent demise—even about her identity. She is represented variously as "a Mrs. Vareck,"[5] "Mrs. Margaretta Van Wyck,"[6] and "Mrs. Margaret Varick."[7] Once source states she came in 1814, another 1817, but both agree it was just after the child's death—which actually occurred on October 1, 1814.[8] Both sources insist the aunt died of a heart attack within three days of her arrival.[9] In fact, the following notice appeared in the *Kentucky Gazette,* August 9, 1817:

> DIED—On the 28th July, at the house of John Brown, Esq. in Frankfort, Mrs. Margaretta Varick, late of New-York, after a short but severe illness.[10]

Here, then, is the identity of the woman presumed to be the Gray Lady—Margaretta Brown apparently having been not only her niece but her namesake as well.

One source, citing "a very interesting tradition handed down in the family," asserts that she died in what is now called the Ghost Room (on the second floor in the house's southwest corner) and "was buried on the grounds." The source continues:

This Lady in Grey is supposed to arise at night and seek her final resting place, but her unsuccessful attempts are attributed to the fact that no grave is found on the grounds and if she was buried here, her remains were later removed to the Frankfort Cemetery, after its establishment, for here her grave is marked.[11]

One wonders—if her grave is indeed "marked"—why that source did not trouble to give her name. In fact, Mrs. Varick's tombstone is not to be found in the Brown family plot nor, apparently, anywhere else in the Frankfort Cemetery (which was incorporated in 1844). Neither is there any record of her burial in the cemetery's files.[12] A search of the earlier Frankfort Cemetery that was in use at the time of Mrs. Varick's death was likewise negative; however, it is now a pathetic site whose stones are little more than rubble (fig. 2), and if Mrs. Varick was buried here her grave can no longer be identified. It is even possible that her remains were removed from the state and buried with family members in New York or Illinois.

Nevertheless, her spirit "nightly haunts" the house according to one writer, who adds: "Only a tale, but the Ghost Lady in Grey has gained recognition far and wide and is held in awe by many people."[13]

Interestingly enough, however, the historical record appears to be silent concerning the Gray Lady for decades after Mrs. Varick's death. Only one source describes the supposed first visitation of the ghost—i.e., the "origination of the expression 'Ghost Room.' " According to the source, Miss Mary Mason Scott, great-granddaughter of John and Margaretta Brown, was at the time "home from finishing school" and occupied the room in which Mrs. Varick had died. Then, "in the dead of night," Miss Scott "ran screaming from the room exclaiming that she had seen a ghost"—a "Lady in Gray" as she described the apparition.[14] Miss Scott, who was born in 1867, would probably have been in her teens at the time (since she was in finishing school). Therefore, the event should have transpired sometime in the 1880s—probably sometime after May 10, 1882, when Miss Scott's mother was deeded the house by her siblings.[15] Thus it would appear that the Gray Lady waited at least sixty-five years before making her first appearance at Liberty Hall.[16]

If true, this account also means that the image of the Gray Lady—if not the Liberty Hall ghost tradition itself[17]—was launched by an impressionable, and apparently quite emotional, schoolgirl (who remained a spinster until her death in 1934). In fact, since the sighting occurred when she was abed, there is every likelihood that she experienced what psychologists term a hypnopompic hallucination, or so-called "waking dream." Such visions are commonly of the ghost-at-the-bedside form.[18]

Moreover, the particular image is such as a young Victorian lady would have been likely to conjure up. In his *Appearances of the Dead: A Cultural History of Ghosts,* skeptic R. C. Finucane demonstrates how people's perceptions of ghosts have altered over time and how each period perceives them in terms of its own cultural attitudes. As he says:

> Each epoch has perceived its specters according to specific sets of expectations; as these change so too do the specters. From this point of view it is clear that the suffering souls of purgatory in the days of Aquinas, the shade of a murdered mistress in Charles II's era, and the silent grey ladies of Victoria's reign represent not beings of that other world, but of this.[19]

Speaking specifically of the Victorian era, Finucane says of the ghostly figures:

> The forms tended to be insubstantial, vague, often in neutral tones of grey and black, or associated with some random luminescence. Many claimed to see a melancholic disposition in the features of their visitors, though this was hardly universal. The best description for the majority of perceptions is "neutral." There seems to be no noticeable bias as between male and female specters, though overall most percipients were women. Certainly most collective observations involved women.

He adds:

As for affect, this varied widely. Some percipients became hysterical, others turned over and went back to sleep; both men and women ran the entire gamut of emotional responses. When it comes to purpose, observers usually attributed no specific reason for the perceptions they reported. *Most* Victorian ghosts were perceived as having nothing to say about buried treasure, murders, revenge, legacies, and *most* percipients evidently felt no need to provide a resolution to this puzzle. The apparition was there; that was enough.[20]

For Victorians, the mere presence of a ghost served to reassure them of their immortality. If they sometimes questioned whether or not there was life after death, Finucane says: "The answer was provided by silent grey ladies who stood at the foot of the bed, and dark nameless figures that floated away without so much as a word."[21]

Fitting precisely this pattern are the sightings at Liberty Hall "of a small, trim woman dressed in gray, usually doing some household chore."[22] For example, "She has been seen sewing or knitting, or walking up the stairs, while many townspeople stoutly maintain they have seen the Gray Lady looking out the palladian window at the front of the house."[23] Not surprisingly, perhaps, the descriptions vary. One from 1940 insists that the apparition is "attired in a gray traveling coat and bonnet and heavily veiled,"[24] while a 1974 description has her wearing "a long, gray silk dress"[25]—ethereal silk, to be sure.

The Evidence

Such sightings have been relatively rare, however. For example, a writer for a Works Progress Administration Project (1935–41) said of the Gray Lady: "Six times she has been seen through the years, the last about ten years ago."[26] And Arthur Myers reports, in his *The Ghostly Register:*

In recent years, the manifestations apparently have not included sightings of an apparition. For example, about twenty years ago, after a fire, a fireman and an employee of a local newspaper remained in the building for three nights to guard against vandals. They reported doors closing behind them and candles being snuffed out by sudden drafts of cool air.[27]

On other occasions, a rocker was occasionally seen "going back and forth by itself."[28]

Such feats need not be attributed to ghosts. Drafts are common to old houses (perhaps especially after a fire) and, together with wind that has found its way through cracked panes and slightly open windows, have been responsible for many supposedly ghostly occurrences. These specifically include doors opening and closing and a child's rocking chair moving by itself.[29]

Another category of ghostly phenomena at Liberty Hall is that of the seemingly teleported object. For example, one day on a tea table in the Ghost Room some gold bracelets supposedly appeared, their origin unknown.[30] Again, one summer morning a tour guide was reportedly unable to find the flag that he raised each day; then he discovered it neatly folded on the floor of the living room.[31]

Investigators are forced to regard such anecdotal evidence as inconclusive at best, especially when—as in these two instances—the reports find their way into print as part of the obligatory annual news-media observance of Halloween. Besides, such incidents may easily have more mundane explanations. As other cases demonstrate, reports of hauntings tend to generate other reports, and pranksters and hoaxers often climb on the bandwagon. For instance, in the wake of spooky shenanigans that supposedly occurred in Toronto's Mackenzie House in the 1960s, a workman encountered a hangman's noose placed over the stairway—an obvious bit of mischief by a co-worker.[32]

Moreover, objects may simply be mislaid when one is distracted by a ring of the telephone or a knock at the door. Since the misplacing goes unremembered, a superstitious person may jump to the conclusion that the ghost was responsible. Questioning by an investigator may simply make the informant defensive, and as a result he or she may buttress a report with exaggerations or even fabricated details.

An interesting occurrence took place in the early 1970s at a time when Eugenia Blackburn, former curator of the Kentucky Historical Society museum, resided in Liberty Hall. As reported in *The Ghostly Register,* on this occasion

> She woke up in the middle of the night and began to think of an old beau who had given her a music box, which she hadn't played for years. Suddenly it came to life, playing "Auld Lang Syne" from beginning to end. This piece was one of several on the music box but was the only one that played. "The next day," Mrs. Blackburn says, "my children came to visit me, and I told them what had happened. They jumped up and down on the floor to see if they could make the music box play by the vibration but it didn't make a noise."[33]

Of course, vibrations are only one possibility, along with a change in temperature (e.g., the box becoming cold in the middle of the night), that might have triggered the mechanism. There would even seem to be the possibility that Mrs. Blackburn was dreaming or experiencing a "waking dream."

Certainly there are implausibilities in the story as we have it. We would have to believe that she awoke for no reason, and—again for no reason—began to think of her former beau; then her thoughts would have to have been divined by the ghost who—for reasons that once again remain elusive—decided to cause the music box to play. (Of course one could dispense with the haunting hypothesis and instead postulate that Mrs. Blackburn generated a psychokinetic—or "mind-over-matter"—influence on the music box, but again proof would be lacking and the existence of psychokinesis has not been scientifically verified.)[34]

Such other reported experiences as feeling a ghostly tap on the shoulder (as a former curator and tour guide each reported to me, albeit the former at second hand),[35] or experiencing "cold spots" in a downstairs rear hallway,[36] or perceiving, as another tour guide reported,[37] that someone was watching him—these are too subjective to be given any credence whatsoever.

Touted as the "most convincing argument" for the reality of the Gray Lady is a color photograph of the front stairway, showing what a journalist described as "a shadowy outline"; he added: "if one looks close enough he can see the bustles of a dress and the outline of an arm reaching for the railing."[38] The photo was made by a former curator, Beulah (Mrs. Robert) Coleman, who recalls that it was taken on a Sunday morning in March 1967 to document restoration work. Unfortunately, she no longer has the camera or is able to recall its type or the kind of film used, but an old news story reported the camera was an Instamatic.[39] Worse, the original negative of this photograph has been lost. Although I was able to locate two different copies of the photo, neither was made from the original negative (see fig. 3).

During the second half of the nineteenth century, when photography was still relatively young, it was commonly believed that cameras were capable of capturing the images of ghosts. One of the earliest photographers to specialize in making spirit pictures was William H. Mumler of Boston. He was exposed as a fraud when the images of living Bostonians, who had earlier had their photos made at Mumler's studio, turned up as "ghosts" in his fake productions.[40] Unfortunately, Mumler represented the rule rather than the exception in spirit photography, prompting one writer to state: "it is a matter of everlasting regret that so many charlatans battened on to the idea and that very little credence is now given to even the most carefully authenticated 'spirit photograph.' "[41]

Fake spirit photos can be make by double exposure, or by rephotographing a pasted-up or otherwise altered print, or other means—twenty-two even by one early count.[42] Also there are those ghostly images that result from accidents: e.g., reflections, or flaws in the camera or the film, or someone entering a scene that was being photographed by a prolonged exposure.[43]

Determining the cause of a photographic anomaly may not always be possible even under the best of conditions, but with the negative missing and only a copy print available, Mrs. Coleman's photo cannot seriously be considered as evidence in the case of the Gray Lady's ghost.

Even so, it was apparent that some people would regard it as such. Therefore, I began a study of the picture, discovering almost at once that it bore a remarkable similarity to another specter-on-the-stairway photo, one of the so-called "Brown Lady" of Raynham Hall in Norfolk, England. That photograph, made in 1936, has been demonstrated a fake, made by superimposing one image over another.[44] Had a prank been played on Mrs. Coleman? She told me she did not witness the ghost, stating, "The picture showed up in one of my batches of negatives and that's all I can tell you."[45]

At my request, a professional photographer, Clint Robertson, agreed to investigate the photograph in question. He subsequently reported:

My first theory on the Ghost of Liberty Hall photograph was that the camera simply malfunctioned. However, if a flash had been used and both camera and flash functioned properly, a normal flash photo would have resulted. A ghost or a person would have to be moving faster than the speed of light to be represented several times in one normal flash exposure.[46]

After considering various other possibilities and performing "several empirical tests to determine whether or not the photograph is a result of a malfunction or darkroom manipulation," Robertson concluded:

It is my experienced and educated photographic opinion that the photograph is, at best, the result of an accident. I am certain for photographic and scientific reasons that the figure ascending the stairs definitely is a person and not an apparition.[47]

Noting that the arm of the ghostly figure extends to the bannister (it is seen as a line of highlight in the photo, repeated several times and thus indicating movement), Robertson asks: "Why should a ghost, an ethereal spirit of the netherworld, have to use a handrail to guide itself to the top of the stairs?"[48]

Analysis

If, as investigation of the legend and examination of the evidence indicates, there is no ghost at Liberty Hall, why does the story persist? Part of the answer lies in the continuing climate of belief in ghosts as seeming to provide proof of immortality. An old house offers a convenient habitat for a spirit, whose imagined existence is kept alive, so to speak, by articles and books that cater to popular superstitions, as well as by a lively oral tradition.

The tale of the Gray Lady was also fostered by well-meaning promoters of tourism, especially one Liberty Hall curator. With the accession of Mrs. Coleman to the position in 1965, the ghost—who was previously confined to the single upstairs chamber, the "Ghost Room"[49]—began to appear elsewhere in the house and to visit more frequently.[50]

In fact, Mrs. Coleman, who retired as curator in 1977, told me:

> There is plenty of history about the place but it is the ghost story that brings the tourists back. The Colonial Dames do a wonderful job of restoration and preservation but it needs money spent on it constantly so it is sensible to try to keep the tourists happy.[51]

Although she says she never saw a ghost herself,[52] she admits that since her retirement, "I continued to tell the ghost story because the new hostess disapproved of ghosts and refuses to tell it."[53]

Like Mrs. Coleman, the new curator, Mary Smith, has not see a ghost. Indeed, she has not experienced any ghostly phenomena during her entire tenure, which extends back to 1977. She told me that she is "skeptical" of all haunting reports, explaining that old houses often yield minor disturbances—make creaking noises, for example—without any ghost being responsible. She mentioned that a rear door, which is kept ajar, sometimes moves back and forth, but that that is due to the wind.[54]

Unlike Mrs. Coleman, however, Mrs. Smith does not feel the need to foster belief in supernatural occurrences. Therefore, while it is still possible to find people who think they have experienced something "strange" in Liberty Hall—some of the elderly folk have stories to tell, as do a few impressionable young people—the ghostly occurrences have clearly diminished in recent years.

This is not surprising. A climate of belief prompts people to experience what they think are otherworldly phenomena. Milbourne Christopher, former head of the Occult Investigation Committee of the Society of American Magicians, who personally investigated many allegedly haunted houses, stated:

> People expect to hear strange noises and see stranger sights in buildings where ghosts are said to walk. The sound of an unseen rat as it scampers across a corridor becomes the scratches of a phantom, a billowing curtain becomes a shrouded woman, a shadow becomes a menacing intruder to those with vivid imaginations.[55]

In other words, it may be that ghosts must be believed to be seen. And so it is that Robert A. Baker, psychologist and noted "ghostbuster," suspects: "There are no haunted houses, only haunted minds."[56]

Notes

1. Arthur Myers, *The Ghostly Register* (Chicago: Contemporary Books, 1986), 130–33; *Liberty Hall/Orlando Brown House* (Lexington, Ky.: Printed for the National Society of the Colonial Dames by Vistacolor Corp., 1989), 8–23; Herbert Sparrow, "The Gray Lady," *State Journal* (Frankfort, Ky.), Oct. 27, 1974.

2. Rebecca K. Pruett, *The Browns of Liberty Hall* (Masonic Home, Ky.: Printed for the National Society of the Colonial Dames of America in the Commonwealth of Kentucky by the Masonic Home Printing Office, 1966), 11–13; *Liberty Hall/Orlando Brown House*, 4–8.

3. Pruett, *The Browns*, 13; *Liberty Hall*, 8.

4. *Liberty Hall*, 8.

5. Typescript headed "Points of Interest—No. 4," in United States Works

Progress Administration (WPA) in Kentucky Records, American Guide Series, 1935–1941, Franklin County (in files of Kentucky Dept. for Libraries and Archives, Public Records Division, Frankfort, Ky.), 1.

6. Typescript headed "Liberty Hall. 218 Wilkinson St.," in WPA files (see n. 5), 3.

7. Myers, *Ghostly Register*, 130.

8. *Liberty Hall*, 8.

9. Sparrow, "Gray Lady"; Myers, *Ghostly Register*, 130–31. (Apparently Myers derived his information from Sparrow, except that he corrected 1814 to 1817.)

10. *Kentucky Gazette*, Aug. 9, 1817.

11. Typescript headed "LIBERTY HALL," in WPA files (see n. 5).

12. Interview with Jim Richardson, director of Frankfort Cemetery Co., Inc., Feb. 14, 1990.

13. "LIBERTY HALL," (see n. 11), 4.

14. "Points of Interest" (see n. 5), 1.

15. *Liberty Hall*, 11, 14.

16. The assertion that Miss Scott's alleged sighting of the ghost was probably the first gains credence from the apparent absence of the story from publications issued between 1817 (the date of Mrs. Varick's death) and the early 1880s (the approximate time of Miss Scott's otherworldly encounter). My search included such standard reference sources as the OCLC computer data base, *Poole's Index to Periodical Literature 1802–1881*, and indexes to the *New York Times* and the Lexington, Ky., newspapers.

17. Two other ghostly traditions are associated with Liberty Hall. One is the spirit of a Spanish opera singer who allegedly attended a party at the Browns' in 1805 but vanished when she wandered into the garden. The other is the ghost of a War of 1812 soldier; he wistfully peers in at a window, supposedly looking for a young woman who visited the Browns and of whom he was enamored. However, although these two ghosts are said to "slightly antedate Mrs. Varick" (Myers, *Ghostly Register*, 132), that seems to be true only in the sense that they are *attributed* to a slightly earlier time. Proof of any historical basis for the singer's disappearance or the soldier's enamoredness is lacking, as is proof that either tale antedates the first appearance of the Gray Lady.

18. Robert A. Baker, Professor of Psychology, lecture on "ghostbusting,"

University of Kentucky, October 30, 1987; Joe Nickell with John F. Fischer, "Haunted Stairs: The Ghost at Mackenzie House," chap. 2 of *Secrets of the Supernatural* (Buffalo, N.Y.: Prometheus Books, 1988), 18.

19. R. C. Finucane, *Appearances of the Dead* (Buffalo, N.Y.: Prometheus Books, 1984), 223.

20. Ibid., 211–12.

21. Ibid., 212.

22. Myers, *Ghostly Register,* 131.

23. Sparrow, "Gray Lady."

24. Eleanor Hume Offutt, "Liberty Hall, Historic Shrine," unidentified clipping dated Sept. 22, 1940.

25. Sparrow, "Gray Lady."

26. "Liberty Hall" (see n. 6), 3.

27. Myers, *Ghostly Register,* 131. See also "Liberty Hall in Frankfort Built in 1796, Hit by Fire," *Lexington Herald* (Lexington, Ky.), Oct. 26, 1965; Sy Ramsey, "Weird Happenings Reported at Frankfort's Liberty Hall," *Lexington Leader,* Nov. 4, 1965.

28. Sparrow, "Gray Lady."

29. Milbourne Christopher, *ESP, Seers & Psychics* (New York: Thomas Y. Crowell, 1970), 166–69.

30. Sparrow, "Gray Lady."

31. "Spirits on the Loose," *State Journal* (Frankfort, Ky.), Oct. 31, 1974.

32. Nickell with Fischer, *Secrets of the Supernatural,* 21. (For a case involving protracted mischief, see Christopher, *ESP, Seers & Psychics,* 164–66.)

33. Myers, *Ghostly Register,* 131–32.

34. C. E. M. Hansel, *ESP: A Scientific Evaluation* (New York: Charles Scribner's Sons, 1966), 153–63.

35. Beulah (Mrs. Robert) Coleman, letter to Joe Nickell, Feb. 26, 1990. (The tour guide requested anonymity.)

36. Ibid.

37. "Spirits on the Loose."

38. Sparrow, "Gray Lady."

39. Coleman to Nickell, Feb. 26, 1990; Beverly Fortune, "Ghost Stories," *Lexington* (Ky.) *Herald,* Oct. 30, 1980.

40. John Mulholland, *Beware Familiar Spirits* (1938; reprint, New York: Scribner, 1979), 147–48.

41. Peter Haining, *Ghosts: The Illustrated History* (Secaucus, N.J.: Chartwell, 1987), 76.

42. C. Vincent Patrick in 1921; cited by Mulholland, *Beware Familiar Spirits,* 149.

43. Daniel Cohen, *The Encyclopedia of Ghosts* (New York: Dorset, 1984), 248–51.

44. John Fairley and Simon Welfare, *Arthur C. Clarke's Chronicles of the Strange and Mysterious* (London: Collins, 1987), 140, 141.

45. Coleman to Nickell, letters of Feb. 26 and Mar. 10, 1990.

46. Clint Robertson, report to Joe Nickell, Jan. 17, 1991.

47. Ibid.

48. Ibid.

49. Shown by clippings in the "Houses" folder of the vertical file, Department of Special Collections, Margaret I. King Library, University of Kentucky; Offutt, "Liberty Hall"; Sue McClelland Thierman, "A Houseful of History," *Courier-Journal Magazine,* Oct. 4, 1959; Mrs. Hal Williams, "Gift Shop in Operation at Historic Liberty Hall," *Lexington Leader,* Aug. 9, 1961; Bettye Lee Mastin, "Ghosts Still Walk at Liberty Hall," *Sunday Herald-Leader,* June 17, 1962. The WPA papers also indicate that formerly only the "Ghost Room" was haunted: See nn. 5, 6, and 10. If the ghost was reported elsewhere in the house prior to 1965, it was certainly to a limited extent.

50. As show by the following examples: Ramsey, "Weird Happenings"; "Monitor Features Liberty Hall Ghosts," *State Journal,* Sept. 22, 1965; Sparrow, "Gray Lady"; "Spirits on the Loose."

51. Coleman to Nickell, Feb. 26, 1990.

52. Ibid.; Sparrow, "Gray Lady."

53. Coleman to Nickell, Feb. 26, 1990. Mrs. Coleman made similar comments to a reporter: see Fortune, "Ghost Stories."

54. Mary Smith, interview by Joe Nickell, Oct. 5, 1989.

55. Christopher, *ESP, Seers & Psychics,* 172.

56. Quoted in Joe Nickell, *The Magic Detectives* (Buffalo, N.Y.: Prometheus Books, 1989), 15.

Select Bibliography

Christopher, Milbourne. *ESP, Seers & Psychics.* New York: Thomas Y. Crowell, 1970. A skeptical explanation of haunted houses and related paranormal phenomena.

Finucane, R. C. *Appearances of the Dead.* Buffalo, N.Y.: Prometheus Books, 1984. A scholarly treatment of ghosts from a cultural standpoint.

Myers, Arthur. *The Ghostly Register.* Chicago: Contemporary Books, 1986. Pages 130–33. An account of the ghost of the Gray Lady at Liberty Hall, Frankfort, Kentucky.

Acknowledgments

In addition to persons mentioned in the text, I am grateful to James T. Moore of Louisville for supplying one copy of the "ghost" photograph, and to Bill Rodgers and Bill Rodgers, Jr., Frankfort, for providing another. Thanks are also due others who assisted in some way, including Caroline Baldwin, Frankfort; Carla Hill, Midway; Jim Prichard, Kentucky State Archives; and the staff of the Margaret I. King Library, University of Kentucky.

3

Assassin's Double

The assassination of President John F. Kennedy on November 22, 1963, continues to attract conspiracy theories. Perhaps none is so incredible as the notion, advanced in a book published in 1977, that Kennedy was killed not by Lee Harvey Oswald, but by a look-alike assassin.

In his book, *The Oswald File,* retired British solicitor Michael Eddowes wrote that he would "endeavor to prove beyond reasonable doubt": that Soviet premier Khruschev ordered the Soviet Secret Police to assassinate President John F. Kennedy; that "the real ex-Marine Lee Harvey Oswald" did not return from the USSR (to which he had defected in 1959) but, instead, a KGB assassin "in 1962 had entered the United States in the guise of Oswald" and committed the act; and finally, that "to avoid the possibility of World War III," a massive cover-up was undertaken, with the "Warren Report" (actually the *Report of the President's Commission on the Assassination of President John F. Kennedy*) being "A declaration of peace and incidentally an admission of defeat."[1]

These are fantastic allegations. For one thing, such a remarkable resemblance between unrelated people would be incredibly rare. It is true that in 1896 and again in 1904, Londoner Adolph Beck was misidentified as the swindler William Thomas, and only the latter's arrest and correct identification kept the unfortuante Beck from serving out a second prison term. However, subtracting a general resemblance and their walrus mustaches, their similarity of appearance was not impressive. And in the most famous case of "unrelated" look-alikes—that of the criminals Will and William West, whose uncanny resemblance helped advance the use of fingerprinting in America—we now know from genetic and documentary evidence that the men were twin brothers, just as a fellow prisoner had alleged all along.[2]

Eddowes's case for two Oswalds was exceedingly weak. He largely based his claim upon some discrepancies in height and scars between Oswald's Marine Corps records and post-1962 official records. He conceded that the fingerprints of the "two" men matched (he had a former Scotland Yard expert make the comparison), but he offered the "theory" that "the KGB had substituted a forged print card in the FBI fingerprint files, the forgery substituting the imposter's prints in place of the ex-Marine's prints."[3]

Where have we heard a similar story? The 1977 movie, and book by the same title, *The Lincoln Conspiracy*,[4] presented a fabulous story of high-level conspiracy to assassinate President Abraham Lincoln. According to the scenario, one Capt. James W. Boyd was brought into the plot. Boyd supposedly bore a remarkable resemblance to John Wilkes Booth (note that their initials are the same), and, allegedly, it was Boyd who was killed and mistakenly identified as Booth. When the War Department discovered the "error"—so the story goes—a cover-up was launched, with Secretary of War Stanton removing an incriminating eighteen pages from Booth's diary. Finally, says the theory, the "real" Booth escaped to Europe!

This fantasy—apparently based on spurious documents—was thoroughly debunked by *Civil War Times Illustrated*. As editor William C. Davis explained:

There is a special technique to this sort of thing. It has been around a long time, and has been used most effectively in recent years by Erich von Däniken in his "Chariots of the Gods" books. The formula is simple. To present a theory that no reputable authority has ever accepted, first attack the authorities. . . . Next must come the hint of a continuing conspiracy to keep the truth from coming out. . . . Next comes the presentation, and with it the repeated and insistent statement of startling revelations, one building upon another. Repetition brings familiarity, and familiarity breeds belief. Finally, when the supposition has been stated often enough, it is accepted as fact, and *presto!* we have spacemen building cities in South America, a voracious triangle of ocean off Bermuda that swallows ships like anchovies, and a massive plot to assassinate Abraham Lincoln and cover up the crime.[5]

I have no data on the sale of Eddowes's book, but I do know that the reviews were mixed. *Publisher's Weekly* urged that it "demanded attention,"[6] but *Library Journal* spoke against the "paranoid conspiracy scenario" and stated: "Geared to exploit the widespread interest in the assassination, this shoddy book is not recommended."[7]

Nevertheless, in 1980, Eddowes was again stumping for his theories and making headlines: "Oswald's Widow Says Briton's Theory Wrong," reads one clipping. By agreeing to Eddowes's request for an exhumation of the body, Marina Oswald Porter said, "I called his bluff."[8] Oswald's brother Robert, on the other hand, sued to halt the exhumation, claiming Eddowes's efforts were merely "continuing action on the part of Michael Eddowes for his own personal gain and to promote a book he has written for sale and distribution to the public."[9] The public was further provoked—perhaps abused—by such articles as one in the tabloid, *Globe,* with its headline proclaiming, "Oswald Is Alive." An accompanying photo showed a dapper Eddowes, wearing a three-piece suit and a hat, resting on one knee, and pointing to the Oswald grave marker with his cane.[10]

Putting such posturing and the "shoddy book" aside, there remained the problem of identifying the man buried in Rose Hill Cemetery. In

1981 Oswald's grave was opened, and a team of distinguished pathologists performed an autopsy on the body it contained.[11] The autopsy revealed that the assassin was indeed Oswald, based on dental records and the fact that a defect on the left mastoid process (the bony prominence behind the ear) was consistent with a mastoidectomy done on Oswald as a young boy.[12] This settled the matter as far as most people were concerned, although the *Globe* hastened to ask, "When Was Oswald's Body Switched?"[13]

In fact, however, Oswald's body had been positively identified some ten months before! I had launched the identification project after seeing the news reports on the controversy, studying Eddowes's book and reading many other books and articles and textbooks, reviewing the Warren Report plus the report of the House Select Committee on Assassination, talking with Robert Oswald and reading his biography of his brother, and consulting a distinguished identification expert. Specifically I proposed (1) to make a positive identification; (2) to do so without recourse to records (including medical and dental records) that could theoretically have been switched; and (3) to make the identification without breaking into the concrete burial vault and intensifying the anguish of the Oswald family. Before I detail my specific approach, however, first some background on identification will be helpful.

Although descriptions of wanted criminals were employed in ancient Egypt, and although the Babylonians and again the Chinese may have made limited use of finger impressions for personal identification, the first really scientific attempt at identification of criminals was made in 1860. In that year a Belgian prison warden named Stevens began taking measurements of criminals' heads, ears, feet, lengths of bodies, and so forth. His imperfect method was abandoned, but by 1882 Alphonse Bertillon had developed an elaborate anthropometrical system that involved tabulating a series of measurements including height, sitting height, length of outstretched arms, length and breadth of head, length of right ear, and other measurements. Bertillon supplemented his system with such additional data as scars, color of eyes, etc., plus full-face and profile photographs. Eventually fingerprinting replaced the cumbersome *bertillonage,* but the French anthropologist's descriptive *portrait parle* (or "word picture": height, weight, color of hair and eyes, etc.) as well as his "mug" photos are still very much in use.[14]

Fingerprints, of course, are the mainstay of identification. Sometimes even a small portion of a single print offers enough ridge characteristics to make a positive identification. In some instances in which there have been too few ridge characteristics, the pattern of tiny pores along the ridges has served as a basis for identification. (This method is known as poroscopy.) Like fingerprints, palmprints and the prints of the soles of the feet have proven valuable many times.

Because no two things in nature are exactly identical, many other methods of identification have served on occasion—lip impressions, for example, as well as bite marks and dental x-rays, to name a few. Criminals who have thought they were being exceedingly clever by wearing gloves have sometimes been convicted when it was shown that gloves in their possession left weave or other texture patterns identical to latent glove prints at the scene of a crime. Although some of these methods of identification are only rarely employed, that does not in the least diminish their validity on those occasions when they can be used.

Frequently in making an identification several suggestive factors— none alone conclusive—must be weighed together, a sort of this-times-that-times-something-else approach. For instance, in a 1949 case a comparison was made between the description of a missing man and that of a badly decomposed body recovered from a river, its head missing and the hands and feet destroyed by the water. Estimated age, height, and weight of the body were similar to that of the missing man, as were portions of dark trousers plus evidence of certain scars and a heart condition. The initials of the missing man were A.H.S.L., but on a clinic card he had used only A.H.S. Finally, ultraviolent light revealed initials A.H.S. on the wallet of the deceased, and the body was identified as that of the missing man.[15]

Now, in the question of identity of whom we shall call the "Dallas Oswald" (the man arrested as the JFK assassin and subsequently shot by Jack Ruby), there is a great deal of data—some of it, as Eddowes observed, conflicting. For example, the autopsy report of the "Dallas Oswald" gives his height as five feet nine inches, whereas Lee Oswald's USMC (United States Marine Corps) medical examination records state seventy-one inches (five feet eleven). Since Eddowes has repeatedly stressed this discrepancy, it is only fair for the reader to learn that an Oswald photo—on his Marine Corps "Miscellaneous Information and Index" record giving his height as sixty-eight inches or five feet eight inches—shows him before a height chart, just reaching the five-nine mark. In other words, whereas Eddowes cites the USMC records as evidence of inconsistency with the autopsy report, the opposite conclusion could be drawn. (Actually, it seems that at this time Oswald was five-eight—his reaching the five-nine mark in the photo being due to his standing slightly away from the chart and closer to the camera.)

It appears that the mature Oswald's height was approximately five feet nine, but that—perhaps out of vanity—he often claimed to be two inches taller and that his word was frequently accepted by those who didn't have a yardstick handy. Eddowes himself mentions that Oswald apparently wore thick-heeled boots,[16] which could transform a five foot nine man into a five-eleven one. And Eddowes is aware of a discrepancy between the descriptions recorded by two different women journalists who had interviewed Oswald in Moscow—one had Oswald as five-nine with brown eyes, the other as five-eleven with blue eyes. As Eddowes concedes, "Although it would appear that they were interviewing two different men, it was, of course, the same man."[17]

Another series of apparent discrepancies concerns Oswald's scars. One behind his left ear, from the mastoidectomy, was recorded in the USMC records (presumably volunteered by Oswald himself) but not noted in the autopsy report. However, the doctors who conducted the postmortem examination were not specifically looking for a mastoidectomy scar (they did not have the USMC records at the time for comparison), and one of them admitted that the scar might have been hidden in the hair. It is also conceivable that this scar, made when Oswald was only six, had become quite faint over the years.

Under the heading, "The Scars on the Left Arm," Eddowes states,

"The postmortem report had disclosed only two scars on the left upper arm of the assassin, whereas there had been three scars on the upper arm of Marine Oswald."[18] Specifically, the USMC "Report of Medical Examination" lists (in addition to the one-inch left mastoid scar) the following: "S operation, 1″ ULA"; "S gunshot, left elbow"; "S ½″ left hand"; and "VSULA" (which might have been added as an afterthought to indicate that the first of the above was a vertical scar). Oswald had accidentally shot himself while in the Marines and a physician had made an incision to remove the missile. The autopsy report notes scars on the upper left arm that appear to be consistent with these two scars, or else they are stunningly coincidental: One is a "somewhat puckered and irregular scar"; the other is "a 1¼ inch *vertical* scar with cross hatching" (my emphasis).[19]

Two other scars noted on the postmortem report are likewise strikingly similar to those of Oswald. One on the back of the left hand was "a poorly defined pale white oblique ½ inch scar" consistent with the "S ½″ left hand" noted above. The other—a transverse scar across the left wrist—was not, as Eddowes notes, recorded on the Marine records for the very understandable reason that it had not yet occurred: it resulted from Oswald's attempt at suicide in Moscow, mentioned by him in his diary and confirmed by USSR medical records. In sum, although there are some explainable omissions of scars on the autopsy report, those that *are* mentioned are consistent with those of Lee Oswald.

Eddowes offers little else to support his "double" theory. He does attempt to convince his readers that the famous "backyard" photos of Oswald holding a rifle and communist newspaper have been tampered with. Some publications did, the Warren Commission learned, retouch their copies before publication, but expert examination has determined that the actual photos are not montages as Eddowes has asserted.[20]

Now, I have mentioned that a *positive* identification of the "Dallas Oswald" can be—and has been made. But before considering this, let us look at other pertinent identification data. We recall, of course, the fact that the fingerprints of the "two" men match. Eddowes says: "There is no easy way to traverse the fingerprint evidence. If the facts that speak for an imposture were not so compelling, it would be logical to accept the evidence of the fingerprints at face value and to accept the Commission's findings—that the assassin was the former Marine, Lee Harvey Oswald."[21] But are Eddowes's "facts" really "so compelling"? I submit that they are not, that the points raised about the height and scars do not go "beyond reasonable doubt." More evidence to the contrary was available.

First, the blood type, "A," of the "Dallas Oswald," noted on the original autopsy report, matched that given on Oswald's Marine medical record. Naturally, this alone would not represent a positive identification, but it is certainly noteworthy.

More compelling is the identification by next-of-kin. On one of the last programs of the 1980 TV series, "Speak Up, America"—on which Marguerite Oswald indicated she knew that the man killed by Jack Ruby was indeed her son—former New Orleans District Attorney Jim Garrison observed, "A mother knows her own son."

During Lee Oswald's stay in the USSR, he wrote several letters to his mother and brother.[22] He and Robert "had been corresponding regularly," especially after his marriage to Marina.[23] Robert Oswald needed no confirmation from handwriting experts that the handwritten letters in fact came from his brother Lee, though, as we shall see, such confirmation there later would be.

Upon Oswald's return to the U.S., after he and Marina stepped off the plane and "just before they reached the gate," says Robert, "Lee caught sight of us and waved."[24] The recognition was mutual. For about a month thereafter, Lee and Marina lived with Robert and his family. Lee Oswald also saw his mother during this time, and the couple subsequently lived with her for another two weeks until Lee secured for himself and Marina their own apartment.

During this brief but intense period of intimate contact, it is clear that Robert Oswald and his mother knew—beyond *any* doubt—that the man who was subsequently arrested and then killed in Dallas was Lee Harvey Oswald.

Robert often talked with his brother when Lee would phone him at his office.[25] On November 22, 1962—exactly one year before the assassination—Robert invited Lee and Marina to a Thanksgiving reunion at which Lee and Robert's half-brother, John Pic, were present.[26] Pic, of course, also recognized Lee.

Eddowes would have us believe "that Marguerite, Robert, and John Pic *accepted* rather than *recognized* the man who returned."[27] He speaks of the "deception" of Robert by the KGB,[28] but of course it may be that any deception is Eddowes's and that it is self-deception.

For the record, Robert, his mother, and Marina each had a conversation with Oswald while he was in custody after the assassination.[29] Following Oswald's death at Parkland Hospital, Robert viewed his body there;[30] and at the graveside at Rose Hill Cemetery, November 25, 1963, the coffin was opened and the body viewed by the family. Robert states specifically that he took "a last, long look at my brother's face."[31]

To return to the matter of Oswald's handwriting, numerous samples of writing by the "Marine Oswald" and those of the "Dallas Oswald" were compared by experts who subsequently testified before the Warren Commission (1964). The various writings were positively identified by both an FBI expert and a Treasury Department examiner as originating from the same individual.

The House committee in turn convened a panel of distinguished, independent document examiners to study again the handwriting samples "purportedly written and signed by Oswald in the last 7 years of his life."[32] The samples represented the pre-USSR period while Oswald was in the Marines; the period when he was in the Soviet Union; and the time from his return to the U.S. to the day of the assassination.

The committee first ascertained "that none [of the experts] had a prior connection with the FBI or the Kennedy case," before assigning them to their task. After a lengthy and detailed study, each expert concluded that documents from the various periods were "all in the handwriting of the same person."[33]

To further investigate the theory of an alleged "second Oswald," the committee convened a panel of photographic experts and forensic anthropologists. The panel was asked the question, "Is there any photographic evidence of an Oswald imposter?"

The panel examined photographs of Oswald "ranging in time from his Marine Corps enlistment to his arrest in Dallas after the assassination." One analysis was "based on 15 indices derived from 16 measurements of the head and face"; and for comparison, photos were included of Oswald's fellow employee, Billy Lovelady, who bore a "strong physical resemblance to Oswald" and who had been "a source of controversy and confusion regarding the 'man in the doorway' photograph." The Lovelady photographs were to provide "a convenient control or yardstick to measure the variation observed in the facial indices derived from the Oswald photographs."

The indices for Lovelady (the closest Oswald "double" yet connected with the case) were quite different from those of the other photos. The experts concluded: "There are no biological inconsistencies in the Oswald photographs examined that would support the theory that a second person, or double, was involved." They added:

> In addition to the analysis of facial indices describe above, other facial features were compared. For example, in the three profile views, the angle of the nasal bridge in relation to the face was 37° in all three cases and the angle between the nasal septum and the facial plane varied by less than 1°. *The ears are relatively distinctive in shape and are strikingly similar in all photographs where they can be examined.* [My emphasis.][34]

The reference—however brief—to the "strikingly similar" ears is most important and paves the way for a further inquiry into the question of identity. In fact, matching of the configurations of the external ears of individuals has been established as a basis for conclusive identification, as we shall now see.

Bertillon, the identification pioneer mentioned earlier, long ago recognized the human ear as a means of identification. In their 1952 text, *Modern Criminal Investigation,* Soderman and O'Connell state: "The ears constitute the most characteristic part of the body next to the patterns of the friction ridges. They remain unaltered from birth until death. In cases where an arrested person has to be identified by photograph they play a deciding role." For example:

An interesting case in which the ears were used for identification purposes was that of the false Grand Duchess Anastasia of Russia. Some years after World War I a woman, after an attempt at suicide in Berlin, Germany, declared herself to be a daughter of the murdered Czar Nicholas. She said she had escaped the execution of the Czar's family in Ekaterinburg, Siberia, had lost her memory as the result of a blow on the head, and after many adventures had finally come to Berlin. She had a superficial similarity to the real Anastasia, but Professor Bischoff, the head of the Scientific Police Institute at Lausanne, Switzerland, established her non-identity by means of the ears—by comparing profile photographs of the impostor and of the real Anastasia.[35]

A distinguished expert in facial features is Jacques Penry, developer of the "PHOTO-FIT" method of producing composite pictures of suspects (which is in use by police departments in many countries). He states: "Although as unique to every face as a fingerprint is unique to each person, the ears have been almost entirely ignored as a means of identification."

He adds: "The ears of mankind in their infinite permutations and combinations of angle, thickness of rim, length, width, position on head, size and shape of lobe, if any, and many other smaller pattern factors are such that *no two people* are likely to have ears which tally exactly in their detail any more than they are likely to have exactly matching fingerprints." (Original emphasis.)

Again Penry states: "Since the ear-pattern is *unique to every person,* its importance in facial identification from photographs cannot be too greatly stressed, especially in cases where a missing person with a doubtful fingerprint record (or none at all) has deliberately tried to alter his facial appearance." (My italics.) Penry goes on to say:

The ironic situation at present, as it has been for centuries, is that the ear-shape, the only feature which can (apart from fingerprints) provide fundamental proof, remains virtually ignored while every other scrap of photographic evidence is microscopically scanned and debated. It is as if a small number of witnesses were most methodically and intensely cross-examined for the evidence they could offer regarding some ambiguous situation, while the star witness holding the key to the matter stood by, mute and ignored.

One further quote from Penry will suffice:

A selection of photographs may well reveal clear views of the ear which, when examined and compared, may decide whether any photographs of faces A, B, C, and D, et cetera—taken at various stages from infancy—are pictures positively of the same person. Such a decision could be conclusive even when time, hardship, illness or artifice have made changes in the face. . . . It may be hoped that at some time not far hence, methods of unraveling problems of identity—both of malefactors and innocent people—will take far more into account the enormous assistance the conclusive ear evidence can provide.[36]

J. W. Osterburg, in his *The Crime Laboratory,* also cites the value of ear identification. He details a rather unique case in which crime scene technicians, dusting a burgled safe for fingerprints, discovered a latent ear impression! Five suspects were rounded up, their ears printed, and one of the five positively identified as the safecracker on the basis of a conclusive match. In notes to his section on ear identification, Osterburg cites a study showing the value of ear comparison for the identification of infants and also lists as a reference the authoritative textbook by A. V. Iannarelli.[37]

Alfred Victor Iannarelli is surely the world's foremost expert in the specialized field of ear identification. Iannarelli has thirty years experience in law enforcement, including experience as a criminal investigator with the U.S. Army Reserves, which, from the first, provided him with a background in the science of identification. Academically, according to an October 1968 article in *Interpol,* he majored in criminology at the University of California (Berkeley) and is a graduate of numerous criminal justice schools throughout the United States. In addition to his B.S. in police science and a subsequent LL.B., he has been an active member of the International Association for Identification, National Sheriffs' Association, Military Police Association, and others.

In November 1949, Iannarelli began a detailed study of the science of ear identification. Over the years he has made numerous contributions to the science, including some practical photographic techniques. As well, he is the pioneer developer of a system of classification that is especially useful in allowing ear photos to be filed systematically, and that is described in his comprehensive and authoritative textbook, *The Iannarelli System of Ear Identification.*[38] In all, Iannarelli has made either physical or photographic examination of over twenty thousand human ears.

Iannarelli's work has been featured in several books, such as *Personal Identification* by Harrison C. Allison,[39] and numerous magazines and journals including *Military Police Journal, Identification News, The National Sheriff*—even such popular magazines as *Reader's Digest.* The July 1964 issue of *Fingerprint and Identification Magazine* stated that Iannarelli's book is "the first one to put [the ear identification] technique on a scientific plane."

At this point let me restate my criteria for answering the question, "Who is buried in Lee Harvey Oswald's grave?" They were (1) to make a positive identification; (2) to do so without recourse to records that could theoretically be switched; and (3) to make the identification without the necessity of exhuming the body. Specifically, as the reader has perhaps guessed, I proposed to use authenticated photographs of the "Marine Oswald" and the "Dallas Oswald"—the authenticity of which photos had been conceded by Eddowes, although he believed they were of different men—and to have an expert determination made on the basis of the external ears. Naturally, I proposed my plan to A. V. Iannarelli.

He wrote in reply on October 1, 1980: "I totally agree with your suggestions insofar as a form of positive identification." In fact, he had previously made a similar suggestion in "a letter to Jerry Pittman, Eddowes' attorney of record in Dallas. . . . To this date I have neither heard from Pittman nor Eddowes." Iannarelli promised, "If you would like to go forward with it [the investigation of identity] I will give you all the support I can since your proposals were well taken."

Subsequently, Mr. Iannarelli studied a variety of photos alleged to be those of Oswald, particularly the photographs in the report of the House Select Committee on Assassinations, Volume 6 ("Photographic Evidence") and in the Warren Report. Iannarelli sent me a copy of a letter he addressed to the Honorable Louis Stokes, former chairman of the committee, in which he reported that he had "made a thorough study of the anatomical structure" of the ears of the Marine Oswald, in comparison with those of the subject arrested in Dallas and identified by fingerprints as Oswald. Iannarelli concluded "that the flesh lines of the Helix Rim, Lobule, Antihelix, Antitragus and Concha" [specific structures of the external ear] were "identical" for the Marine Oswald and the alleged double.

He also stated: "My total interest in this case is to set the record straight that there is no doubt that the individual arrested, photographed, and identified as Lee Harvey Oswald by the Dallas Police Dept. on November 23, 1963, for the investigation of President Kennedy's murder is indeed the deceased, Mr. Lee Harvey Oswald."[40]

I feel that Mr. Iannarelli deserves the praise of everyone who is sincerely interested in the truth as regards the question of Oswald's identity. His willingness to tackle the problem—without thought of personal gain—is exemplary.

And his expertise in ear identification—which is well established as a means for positively identifying individuals—has put to rest a troubling question of our time. Some may say they "knew it all along," but for them, and others, it can never hurt to have the evidence—evidence that, unlike that presented by Michael Eddowes, is indeed "beyond reasonable doubt."

Of course, questions about the assassination of President Kennedy persist, and conspiracy theories abound. Evidence once believed to indicate two assassins—i.e., Oswald firing from the rear, from a sixth-floor window of the Texas School Book Depository, and another gunman shooting from the front, from the area known as "the grassy knoll"—has been discredited. This evidence includes the sound recording that supposedly registered an extra grassy-knoll shot,[41] the motion-picture frames of the Zapruder film that showed Kennedy's head snapping backward in a manner supposedly proving a frontal shot,[42] and the evidence purportedly discrediting the sarcastically dubbed "super-bullet theory" (i.e., that one of the bullets that struck Kennedy also produced the wounds in Governor John Connally yet remained relatively intact).[43]

In an excellent summary of the years of speculation, Jacob Cohen, in an article titled "Conspiracy Fever,"[44] states:

> One would think that such tension would welcome the relief of decisive resolution. And if ever a question of fact has been resolved it is this one. Late in 1966, the Kennedy family relinquished the autopsy materials to the National Archives, placing strict restrictions on access to them. In February 1968, a panel of four prominent physicians, three forensic pathologists, and a radiologist, each nominated by a prominent person outside of government, was convened by Attorney General Ramsey Clark to review that material and the panel unanimously confirmed every conclusion of the autopsy including the location of the back wound and the evidence of its passage to the throat. They found evidence of no other wounds except those which could have been caused by a gunman above and behind the President.[45]

Concludes Cohen:

> The public . . . never judges issues on their merits—having neither the time, inclination, opportunity, nor ability—but rather forms its conclusions from the sound and style of the debate and its brute sense of the plausible. When the Gallup poll finds, as it has consistently since late 1966, that two-thirds and more of the American public doubt the essential conclusions of the Warren Commission, that only means that many people have heard an ill-mannered debate raging and

concluded that such passionate and apparently well-informed dissent must signify something. After all, where there is smoke there is fire. But the smoke in this case is only the smoke of verbal battle, a green, chemically produced mist not at all like the black billows which arise from real flames. What is alarming is that the public seems incapable of detecting the difference because its sense of the plausible has come to include incredible charges of government wrong-doing.[46]

Notes

1. Michael Eddowes, *The Oswald File* (New York: Clarkson N. Potter, 1977), 1–2.

2. Joe Nickell, "The Two 'Will Wests': A New Verdict," *Journal of Police Science and Administration* 8, no. 4 (Dec. 1980): 406–413.

3. Eddowes, *Oswald File,* 139.

4. David Balsiger and Charles E. Sellier, Jr., *The Lincoln Conspiracy* (Los Angeles: Schick Sunn Classic, 1977).

5. William C. Davis, editorial, *Civil War Times Illustrated,* Aug. 1977: 33–37.

6. *Publisher's Weekly,* Aug. 1, 1977, 108.

7. *Library Journal,* Nov. 15, 1977, 2342.

8. Associated Press, Aug. 17, 1980.

9. Associated Press, Aug. 15, 1980.

10. "Oswald Is Alive," *Globe,* Oct. 21, 1980.

11. The experts were Dr. Linda Norton, an associate professor of pathology at the West Virginia University medical school; Dr. James A. Cottone, University of Texas Health Science Center at San Antonio; and Dr. Vincent DiMaio, medical examiner for Bexar County (Antonio).

12. Dan Balz, "Body in Oswald's Grave Is Oswald's," *Washington Post,* reprinted in the *Louisville Courier-Journal,* Oct. 5, 1981; Linda E. Norton et al., "The Exhumation and Identification of Lee Harvey Oswald," *Journal of Forensic Sciences* 29, no. 1 (Jan. 1984): 19–38.

13. "When Was Oswald's Body Switched?" *Globe,* Oct. 27, 1981.

14. For a brief history of identification see Henry Soderman and John J. O'Connell, *Modern Criminal Investigation* (New York: Funk & Wagnalls,

1952), 68–98.

15. Ibid., 103.

16. Eddowes, *Oswald File*, 41–43.

17. Ibid., 24–25.

18. Ibid., 133.

19. This report—together with other records relating to Oswald—is included in *Report of the President's Commission on the Assassination of President John F. Kennedy* (the "Warren Report").

20. Eddowes, *Oswald File*, 117–19. See also the *Hearings Before the Select Committee on Assassinations*, 1979, vol. 6, 138–215.

21. Eddowes, *Oswald File*, 137.

22. "Warren Report," 689–713.

23. Robert L. Oswald, *Lee: A Portrait of Lee Harvey Oswald by His Brother* (New York: Coward-McCann, 1967), 112.

24. Ibid., 116.

25. Ibid., 126.

26. Ibid., 130–31.

27. Eddowes, *Oswald File*, 37.

28. Ibid., 38.

29. Oswald, *Lee*, 143.

30. Ibid., 152.

31. Ibid., 164.

32. House Select Committee on Assassinations, *Appendix to Hearings*, 95th Congress, 2nd Session, vol. 8 (Mar. 1979), 225.

33. Ibid., 247.

34. Ibid., vol. 6, 273–81.

35. Soderman and O'Connell, *Modern Criminal Investigation*, 97.

36. Jacques Penry, *Looking at Faces and Remembering Them: A Guide to Facial Identification* (London: Elek Books, 1971), 82–92.

37. J. W. Osterburg, *The Crime Laboratory* (Bloomington: Indiana University Press, 1968), 34–35.

38. Alfred V. Iannarelli, *The Iannarelli System of Ear Identification* (New York: The Foundation Press, 1964).

39. Harrison C. Allison, *Personal Identification* (Boston: Holbrook Press, 1973).

40. Alfred V. Iannarelli, letter to Hon. Louis Stokes, Chairman, House

Select Committee on Assassinations, Dec. 5, 1980.

41. Warren E. Leary, "Recordings the Day of JFK Shooting Don't Prove a Conspiracy, Study Says," *Louisville Courier-Journal,* May 15, 1982. (The study was conducted by the National Academy of Sciences and discredited two earlier studies.) See also Bruce E. Koenig, "Acoustic Gunshot Analysis: The Kennedy Assassination," *FBI Law Enforcement Bulletin* 52, no. 11.

42. Luis W. Alvarez, "Physicist Examines the Kennedy Assassination Film," *American Journal of Physics* 44, no. 9 (Sept. 1976): 813–27.

43. "Who Shot President Kennedy?" a "Nova" program narrated by Walter Cronkite, May 18, 1989.

44. Jacob Cohen, "Conspiracy Fever," *Commentary,* Oct. 1975, 33–42.

45. Ibid., 34–35.

46. Ibid., 41.

Selected Bibliography

Eddowes, Michael. *The Oswald File.* New York: Clarkson N. Potter, 1977. Conspiratorial view that President John F. Kennedy was assassinated not by Lee Harvey Oswald, but by a Soviet "double."

Norton, Linda E., et al. "The Exhumation and Identification of Lee Harvey Oswald." *Journal of Forensic Sciences* 29, no. 1 (January 1984): 19–38. Forensic report proving that it was indeed Oswald in Oswald's grave.

Roberts, Charles. *The Truth About the Assassination.* New York: Grosset & Dunlap, 1967. An eyewitness *Newsweek* reporter's point-by-point response to Kennedy-assassination conspiracy theorists.

Acknowledgments

I am supremely grateful to Alfred V. Iannarelli for once again assisting me by applying his unique expertise in ear identification to the solution of an important historical mystery. I also wish to acknowledge the assistance of the staff of the Margaret I. King Library, University of Kentucky, particularly its government records department.

4

The Legend of Beale's Treasure

According to some curious documents known as the Beale Papers, a fabulous bonanza lies in wait for whoever can unlock their mysteries and divine the path to the lost hoard.[1] Or could it be that the entire affair is merely some clever hoax, related, perhaps, to the secret rituals of the Freemasons?[2] The answer lies in the legendary papers, which tell a tale of western adventure, of buried treasure, and of strange ciphers that no one, apparently, can solve.

In 1817, according to the story, a Virginia adventurer named Thomas Jefferson Beale assembled a company of thirty comrades to hunt buffalo and grizzlies in the western frontier. By the next year, some three hundred miles north of Santa Fe, the adventurers accidentally discovered a fabulous lode of gold and silver. Of course, this was more than three decades before the great gold rush brought thousands of easterners swarming to the California coast.

As Beale reportedly wrote in a subsequent letter, to facilitate working the strike he determined "to systematize our operations and reduce everything to order." As he continued:

> With this object in view an agreement was entered into to work in common, as joint partners, the accumulations of each one to be placed in a common receptacle, and each be entitled to an equal share of the whole whenever he chose to withdraw it; the whole to remain under my charge until some other disposition of it was agreed upon.
>
> Under this arrangement the work progressed favorably for eighteen months or more, and a great deal of gold had accumulated in my hands, as well as silver, which had likewise been found. Everything necessary for our purposes and for the prosecution of the work had been obtained from Santa Fe, and no trouble was experienced in procuring assistance from the Indians in our labors.
>
> Matters went on thus until the Summer of 1819, when the question of transferring our wealth to some secure place was frequently discussed. It was not considered advisable to retain so large an amount in so wild and dangerous a locality, where its very possession might endanger our lives; and to conceal it there would avail nothing, as we might at any time be forced to reveal its place of concealment.[3]

Finally the men resolved to transport their treasure by wagon to Virginia's Blue Ridge Mountains, to a secret location near Buford's Tavern in Bedford County. There "in an excavation or vault six feet below the surface of the ground," the vault being "roughly lined with stone,"[4] the adventurers lodged their treasure in iron pots. It was deposited in two installments and consisted of 2,921 pounds of gold and 5,100 pounds of silver, as well as "jewels obtained in St. Louis to save transportation," which were priced at $13,000. At today's value the treasure would be worth an estimated $30 million.[5]

The "company" now devised a contingency plan that they entrusted to one Robert Morriss of Lynchburg. Should some accident befall them, Morriss was to distribute the wealth to their families. Therefore, Morriss was given a strongbox along with instructions that he was not to open it for ten years. Inexplicably, he waited more than twice that long—

a surprising twenty-three years—before unlocking the box and discovering its contents: three papers written in cipher together with an explanatory letter.[6]

One cipher allegedly detailed the vault's contents; another its precise location; and the third a roster of the company, including the names and addresses of each man's relatives and friends. However, Morriss never received the promised key to the cryptograms.

Supposedly, Morriss failed to decipher the papers but, a year before his death in 1863, he passed them (together with two additional letters from Beale to him) on to one James B. Ward of Lynchburg. By "accident," Ward was able to solve one of the ciphers, thus learning the vault's contents, but he could not solve the other ciphers. Eventually, he wrote:

> In consequence of the time lost in the above mentioned investigation I have been reduced from comparative affluence to absolute penury, entailing suffering upon those it was my duty to protect; and this, too, in spite of their remonstrances. My eyes were at last opened to their condition and I resolved to sever at once, and forever, all connection with the affair, and retrieve, if possible, my errors. To do this, and as the best means of placing temptation beyond my reach, I determined to make public the whole matter, and shift from my shoulders my responsibility to Mr. Morriss.[7]

Ward published his pamphlet in 1885, stating, "I anticipate for these papers a large circulation."[8] However, a fire at the Virginia Job Print plant destroyed most of the pamphlets, together with, supposedly, the "original" documents.[9]

Early in this century, two brothers, Clayton and George L. Hart, Sr., took up the challenge to solve cipher number one (see fig. 4) and discover the Beale treasure. The Hart brothers secured the aid of a young medium, whom Clayton—an amateur mesmerist—practiced hypnotizing and who "gradually drifted into crystal reading."[10] The entranced lad told "a wonderful story" and, after many hours of difficult digging at a spot he identified, the brothers struck a hollow-sounding rock. Then:

After awhile we succeeded in removing the rock, but the hoped-for pots of gold and silver were not underneath it. Now, were we let down? To relieve our chagrin the subject was again hypnotized and asked to reveal the whereabouts of the treasure. Rising on the balls of his feet, as if in disgust, he pointed to the left about two feet, directly underneath the great oak tree, and exclaimed: "There it is! You got over too far! Can't you see it?"

Soon, George's interest in the matter waned, but Clayton continued his quest for the Beale treasure until his death in 1949.[11]

Others have followed in droves, the perpetual search being termed "one of the longest and costliest treasure hunts in U.S. history."[12] Enlisting the aid of such diverse devices as computers, metal detectors, dowsing pendulums, and backhoes, treasure hopefuls have pursued the elusive goal with often tragicomical results.

A number of treasure hunters, by "forcing" various aspects of the ciphers, often making gigantic leaps of logic and indulging in wishful thinking, have come to what they consider to be positive conclusions. Some have been so sure they have invested large sums of money, digging holes in Virginia real estate (one got permission and dug through the basement of a Roanoke building—to no avail). Some have even purchased land in the region, convinced of the presence of the treasure, and found themselves with just farm land on their hands, albeit well ploughed after their efforts.

Jack Craig of Bedford County tells the story of digging up a sizeable parcel of land with a backhoe for a Tennessee banker in 1966, and the only gold that appeared was the money exchanged for Mr. Craig's labor. On Purgatory Mountain near Buchanan, he more recently employed a bulldozer to level an entire hill for another hopeful; the only result was a relocated hill.[13]

Unfortunately, for those who have succumbed to the Beale mania, the treasure tale is riddled with implausibilities; the text of the documents is filled with errors and anachronisms; and there are Masonic elements that suggest the story may be nothing more than an allegory relating to that secret society.

The implausibilities begin with the unlikelihood that thirty men who discovered such a remarkable lode far in advance of the 1849 gold rush would have been able to keep the secret for so long; that they would have felt the need to bury their valuables communally or produce the encripted messages; or that they would utterly disappear without ever occasioning any notice among their acquaintances and kinfolks, who would surely have publicly expressed their concern.

In fact, specific errors indicate the tale is apocryphal, penned long after the events the papers purport to record as contemporary occurrences. For example, Morriss's alleged account begins, "It was in the month of January, 1820, while keeping the Washington Hotel, that I first saw and became acquainted with Beale"—who supposedly lodged with him that winter. Unfortunately for the account's credibility, Morriss did not become proprietor of the Washington Inn until almost four years later, as shown by the following notice from the *Lynchburg Virginian* of December 2, 1823:

Washington Inn

The subscriber informs his friends and the public in general, that he has rented the house known by the above name, situated on Third Street . . . and he is now prepared to accommodate BOARDERS, and TRANSIENT CUSTOMERS. . . .

Robert Morriss.

Again, in the April 17, 1826, issue, Morriss notified the public:

The subscriber has moved from the Washington, which he has occupied *for more than two years past* [emphasis added], to the Franklin Hotel. . . .

Robert Morriss.

Moreover, the Washington Inn was not called the Washington *Hotel* until after Morriss ceased to be its proprietor.[14]

In addition, certain words in the Beale Papers date from later times. For instance, Beale's letter dated January 4, 1822, mentions "stampeding" a herd of buffalo.[15] However, according to authoritative sources, the root word *stampede* (from the Spanish *estampida*) apparently did not enter into print before 1844, and the earliest known printed use of *stampeding* dates from 1883—only two years prior to publication of Ward's pamphlet.[16]

Actually, there is no proof that the putative author of the Beale Papers even existed. Beales abound, of course, including those with the common name Thomas, as revealed by a computer-generated search for the Beale surname in early nineteenth-century records that I commissioned.[17] However, despite various attempts, no one has yet proven that there was a Thomas Jefferson Beale who early discovered gold in California. For example, one researcher, who came across a mention of one "Thomas Beall" in an 1820 Missouri newspaper, nevertheless "has found no conclusive evidence that Beale was where he said he was at the time. On the other hand, he has found no evidence that he was not. . . ."[18] Of course, it may be well to point out, the burden of proof is always on the advocate of an idea or an asserter of fact.[19]

Since the evidence indicates that Beale is fictitious and the tale is of 1880s vintage, James Ward becomes an obvious suspect in the hoax. That he claimed to have solved one of the ciphers magnifies the suspicion. (Having consecutively numbered the words of the Declaration of Independence, Ward then matched a given number in cipher two with the corresponding number in the declaration.) As the noted cryptanalyst George Fabyan wrote in 1925:

> It seems improbable to us that a cipher of this character could be deciphered by a novice without the key, regardless of whether he put 20 years or 40 years on it. The cipher would be classified as a complex substitution cipher—variable-key system, or pseudo code, and even though one were told that the Declaration of Independence was the

key, unless it was intimated as to how it was used as a key, we think that the novice would have been utterly baffled as to how to use it. The stumbling of a novice upon a method of this character lies rather beyond the range of possibility, and the conviction follows that they were in possession of the key of not only No. 2, but also of No. 1 and No. 3.[20]

To test the hypothesis that Ward fabricated the documents, I applied stylometric analysis to the problem. Stylometry involves "looking at habits which are common to all writers of the class under examination. The habits are used by each writer at his own rate. The different writers are separated by calculating the differences between their rates."[21] For controls, sample writings of other nineteenth-century Virginians were used: Chief Justice John Marshall, John Randolph of Roanoke, and Ward contemporary John Randolph Tucker. The result was that striking stylometric similarities between Beale and Ward were demonstrated.

A follow-up analysis, a more traditional linguistic study, was done by Prof. Jean G. Pival of the University of Kentucky, a specialist in English linguistics and rhetoric. Her analysis (reported in detail else-where)[22] is summarized in the following table:

	Negatives	Negative Passives	Infinitives	Relative Clauses
Beale	24	6	44	30
Ward	36	7	40	39
Marshall	15	0	21	8
Randolph	29*	0	18	9
Tucker	14	0	16	34

*Ten of the negatives occur in one letter, in which Randolph tries to justify his participation in a duel.

Professor Pival concluded, as a result of her analysis:

If it is true, as many linguists claim, that any individual's writing style is characterized by idiosyncratic choice of the various syntactical options available in language, then the striking similarities in the Ward and Beale documents argue that one author was responsible for both. Although two writers might share one idiosyncratic characteristic, the sharing of several extraordinary features constitutes, I think, conclusive evidence that the same hand wrote both documents.[23]

Where did Ward get the idea for the hoax? Such storybook elements as the Beale Papers contain are reminiscent of other tales about cryptic documents that point to lost treasure. For instance, P. B. and Walter Dean Innis state, in their *Gold in the Blue Ridge: The True Story of the Beale Treasure*:

Some people have suggested that Edgar Allan Poe's tale, "The Gold Bug," was based on the Beale treasure story, but as the code used in "The Gold Bug" is quite a different type, there seems no reason to link the two. It is a well known fact that Poe was haunted by bitter poverty all his life so he could not have found the treasure.[24]

But the Innises are missing the essential point, that the historical record places Poe's story decades before the Beale one, which was not published prior to 1885 and—so far as can be determined—has absolutely no provenance before that time.

A more telling precursor story would seem to be that of Swift's Silver Mines, a Kentucky legend dating from the late-eighteenth century.[25] The Swift tale likewise features a "company" of men who discover and then conceal a great treasure; it, too, remains lost—despite a "journal" that provides cryptic directions to the reputed mines. In addition, the journal appears to have been accompanied by a map (since lost) that seems to "have been in cipher."[26]

Like "Beale," "Swift" has never been proved to have existed, and there are numerous Masonic elements throughout the "journal." These invite interpreting the story as a Freemasons' allegory of the "secret vault"—a legendary repository of lost secrets. For example, at one point Swift claims he marked a tree with "the symbols of a compass [some versions read "compasses"], trowel and square"—Masonic symbols, certainly.[27] Again, he states that, when he left the "richest mine" for the last time, he "walled it up with masonry form." This otherwise unlikely statement appears to affirm that the meaning has been concealed in Masonic fashion.[28]

Now Masonry has been defined as "a peculiar system of morality veiled in allegory and illustrated by symbols."[29] Among the essential elements of any genuine Masonic group are "a legend or allegory relating to the building of King Solomon's temple" and "symbolism based on the stonemason's trade."[30] Thus the Swift story could have been intended to evoke Solomon's fabled mines; numerous other references, e.g., to "monument rocks,"[31] could be similarly suggestive. For instance, Swift's smelting furnace being in a "rockhouse that faces the east"[32] calls to mind the Masonic significance of facing the east.[33]

When "Swift" later becomes blind and thus unable to relocate his hoard, the story is reminiscent of the fact that Masonic applicants are initially required to enter the lodge like Swift—in *complete blindness.*[34] This detail underscores the moral of the allegory: the futility of "laying up treasures."

The Beale story is obviously quite similar and likewise contains Masonic elements. For instance "Beale" states that his company of men discovered their gold "in a cleft of the rocks."[35] This distinctive expression will be immediately recognized by Master Masons as coming from the rite of the third degree. As one Masonic glossary explains:

CLEFTS OF THE ROCKS. The whole of Palestine is very mountainous, and these mountains abound in deep clefts or caves, which were anciently places of refuge to the inhabitants in time of war, and were often used as lurking places for robbers. It is, therefore, strictly in accordance with geographical truth that the statement, in relation to the concealment of certain persons in the clefts of the rocks, is made in the third degree.[36]

Again, when Beale uses the term "vault" to describe his treasure trove,[37] the equation with Masonry's allegorical "secret vault" seems intentional. The latter concerns King Solomon's subterranean depository of certain great secrets, and the Masonic rites of the Master Mason feature a quest after such vague secrets: specifically, "that which is lost," which—in the end—remains lost.[38] That is the obvious plot of the Beale treasure story.

In cipher number two, the solved cipher, Beale said he had "deposited" the treasure in its vault. This evokes the ritual of the ninth, or Select Masters', degree, wherein the Right Illustrious Master states:

> Thrice Illustrious, it is my most ardent wish to see the secret vault completed and the sacred treasures therein safely deposited, that I may return to my own country with the satisfaction of having faithfully performed my duties to the craft.[39]

That the vault was "roughly lined with stones" and that the treasure-containing vessels were said to "rest on solid stone" are details that are further suggestive of Masonry and its requisite "symbolism based on the stonemason's trade" (as mentioned earlier). Moreover, in the Royal Arch Degree, the concept of striking stone to see whether it is hollow or solid is the means of locating the Secret Vault.[40] The roughness of the stones may suggest the Masonic *rough ashlar*—a stone in its rude state, as taken from the quarry, and reminiscent of man's imperfect natural state.[41]

Of course, if the Masonic symbolism was intentional, it would suggest that James Ward was probably a Freemason. Indeed Ward's record of membership in "Dove Lodge No. 51" shows that he became an Entered Apprentice on December 6, 1862—the year he claimed Morriss gave him the secret papers![42] He became a Master Mason on November 9, 1863, but was "suspended" on October 25, 1867. No further details are given, but that term is distinguished in the records from the following other designations: "expelled," "rejected," "reinstated," "withdrawn," and "died."[43] Suspension might indicate nothing more sinister than non-payment of dues.

Little is known about James Ward. His neighbors accorded him respect,[44] and one researcher labeled him "a gentleman of independent means," without supplying further details.[45] Ward said little about himself in his pamphlet except that he had worked at deciphering the papers to the neglect of his family and friends "and all legitimate pursuits for • what has proved, so far, the veriest illusion." Eventually "absolute want" forced him, he alleged, to abandon the task.

The motivation behind Ward's hoax remains uncertain. Despite his "absolute want," and his anticipation of "a large circulation" for the pamphlets, he could scarcely have believed he could become wealthy selling them at fifty cents apiece. Moreover, the opinions of his neighbors urge us to set aside any very sinister motive.

Indeed, Ward seemed genuinely to admire the virtues he saw in Robert Morriss, stating:

> It was not the wealthy and distinguished alone who appreciated Mr. Morriss. The poor and lowly had blessings for the man who sympathized with their misfortunes, and was ever ready to relieve their distress. Many poor but worthy families, whose descendants are now in our midst, can remember the fact that his table supplied their daily food, not for days and weeks only, but for months at a time.[46]

Benevolence versus greed is a theme characterizing the Beale Papers. Freemasonry is a benevolent society, ministering to the "spiritually as well as the financially poor and distressed," and we note Ward's use of the word "distress"—an important one in Masonry.[47]

So clear are the Masonic overtones in the Beale Papers that the Innises state (albeit missing the essential point once again):

> It is believed by some people that Thomas Jefferson Beale was a third degree Mason of the Scottish rite and the secret of the codes can only be discovered by another Mason, because Beale and his party wanted to safeguard their families and a brother Mason would see that this was done.[48]

Actually, of course, Beale and his treasure are illusory—merely part of an allegory meant to evoke the anticipated Masonic "discovery of the secret vault and the inestimable treasures, with the long-lost word" (as expressed in the Royal Arch degree).[49] The contrast between the futile quest for gold and that for more spiritual wealth are didactically expressed in the allegory. Ward did state in his pamphlet that he was publishing the ciphers "with the hope that all that is dark in them may receive light"[50]—the concept of "light out of darkness" (*lux e tenebris*) being an essential Masonic one.[51] Whether more will yet come to light remains to be seen.

Notes

1. James B. Ward, *The Beale Papers containing Authentic Statements regarding the Treasure Buried in 1819 and 1821, near Buford's in Bedford County, Virginia and which Has Never Been Recovered* (Lynchburg, Va.: privatedly printed, 1885); this pamphlet is reprinted as "The Beale Papers" in P. B. Innis and Walter Dean Innis, *Gold in the Blue Ridge: The True Story of the Beale Treasure* (Washington, D.C.: Robert B. Luce, 1973), 131–76.

2. This thesis was first set forth in Joe Nickell, "DISCOVERED: The Secret of Beale's Treasure," *Virginia Magazine of History and Biography* 90, no. 3 (July 1982): 310–24.

3. Beale's alleged letter—to Robert Morriss, January 4, 1822—is given in Ward's pamphlet; see Innis and Innis, *Gold in the Blue Ridge*, 145–52.

4. The description of the vault and other details are given in one of Beale's alleged ciphers, which Ward claimed to have solved and which will be discussed presently.

5. Louis Kruh, "A Basic Probe of the Beale Cipher as a Bamboozlement," *Cryptologia* 6 (Oct. 1982): 378.

6. Alleged statement of Robert Morriss in Ward's pamphlet: Innis and Innis, *Gold in the Blue Ridge*, 138–40.

7. Ward in ibid., 175. (He uses the ploy that another who wishes to remain anonymous is speaking, and that he is merely the publisher of the account. However, researchers who spoke with Ward and his son about 1903,

and virtually all subsequent authorities, have concluded Ward was indeed the author of the pamphlet. See Innis and Innis, *Gold in the Blue Ridge,* 11, 128, 181; see also Robert Flanagan, "Gold in Our Hills," *Country,* Feb. 1982, 32.)

8. Ibid.

9. Innis and Innis, *Gold in the Blue Ridge,* 128, 208–209.

10. George L. Hart, Sr., "The Hart Papers," in Innis and Innis, *Gold in the Blue Ridge,* 179–201.

11. Ibid., 184–85.

12. "NBC Magazine," television program, Oct. 23, 1981.

13. Flanagan, "Gold in Our Hills," 32–33.

14. See Nickell, "DISCOVERED," 315.

15. Innis and Innis, *Gold in the Blue Ridge,* 148.

16. Sir William Draigie and James Hulbert, eds., *A Dictionary of American English on Historical Principles* (Chicago: University of Chicago, 1944); and Mitford M. Mathews, ed., *A Dictionary of Americanisms on Historical Principles* (Chicago: University of Chicago, 1951). For another example and a more detailed discussion, see Nickell, "DISCOVERED," 316–17.

17. Nickell, "DISCOVERED," 312–13.

18. Ruth Daniloff, "A Cipher's the Key," *Smithsonian* 12, no. 1 (1981): 127–28.

19. David A. Binder and Paul Bergman, *Fact Investigation: From Hypothesis to Proof* (St. Paul: West, 1984), 13; see also Joe Nickell, *Literary Investigation: Texts, Sources, and "Factual" Substructs of Literature and Interpretation,* Ph.D. dissertation, University of Kentucky, 1987, 8.

20. George Fabyan, letter to George L. Hart, Sr., Feb. 3, 1925; this excerpt appeared in "The Hart Papers" (see Innis and Innis, *Gold in the Blue Ridge,* 186).

21. A. Q. Morton, *Literary Detection: How to Prove Authorship and Fraud in Literature and Documents* (New York: Scribner's, 1978), 38.

22. Prof. Jean G. Pival, report to Joe Nickell, Nov. 1981; given in Nickell, "DISCOVERED," 321–22.

23. Ibid., 322.

24. Innis and Innis, *Gold in the Blue Ridge,* 210.

25. See Joe Nickell, "Uncovered—The Fabulous Silver Mines of Swift and Filson," *Filson Club History Quarterly* 54 (Oct. 1980): 325–45.

26. Ibid., 345, n. 91.

27. Swift's "journal," as given in Michael Paul Henson, *John Swift's Lost Silver Mines* (Louisville, Ky.: privately printed, 1975), 16.

28. Ibid., 22.

29. *Masonic Heirloom Edition Holy Bible* (Wichita, Kans.: Heirloom Bible Publishers, 1964), 26.

30. *Collier's Encyclopedia*, 1978, under "Freemasonry."

31. "Journal," *Lost Silver Mines*, 17.

32. Ibid.

33. Ralph P. Lester, ed., *Look to the East!* (rev. ed.; Chicago: Ezra A. Cook Publications, 1977); *Masonic Bible*, 10.

34. Lester, *Look to the East!* 26

35. Beale to Morriss, Jan. 4, 1822 (Innis and Innis, *Gold in the Blue Ridge*, 148).

36. Albert G. Mackey, *A Lexicon of Freemasonry* (Philadelphia: Moss & Co., 1866), 89; see also *Masonic Bible*, 37.

37. Beale, cipher two (Innis and Innis, *Gold in the Blue Ridge*, 170–71).

38. For a brief explanation of the "secret vault," see *Revised Knight Templarism Illustrated* (Chicago: Ezra A. Cook, 1975), 64, n. 22.

39. *Revised Knight Templarism Illustrated*, 64.

40. Malcolm C. Duncan, *Masonic Ritual and Monitor* (Chicago: Ezra A. Cook, 1972), 242.

41. *Cross' Masonic Chart, Revised* (Philadelphia: Moss & Co., 1865), 28.

42. Ward, in Innis and Innis, *Gold in the Blue Ridge*, 136–37.

43. Fred W. Troy (Deputy Grand Secretary of the Grand Lodge), letter to Joe Nickell, Apr. 16, 1980 (including photocopy of Ward's record).

44. Hart, in Innis and Innis, *Gold in the Blue Ridge*, 187.

45. Daniloff, "Cipher's the Key," 131.

46. Ward, in Innis and Innis, *Gold in the Blue Ridge*, 135.

47. Robert Macoy, *General History, Cyclopedia and Dictionary of Freemasonry* (New York: Macoy, 1871), 489.

48. Innis and Innis, *Gold in the Blue Ridge*, 220.

49. Duncan, *Masonic Ritual and Monitor*, 252.

50. Ward, in Innis and Innis, *Gold in the Blue Ridge*.

51. Robert Macoy, *Illustrated History and Cyclopedia of Freemasonry* (New York: Macoy, 1908), 530.

Select Bibliography

Innis, P. B., and Walter Dean Innis. *Gold in the Blue Ridge: The True Story of the Beale Treasure.* Washington, D.C.: Robert B. Luce, 1973. Account of the Beale treasure legend along with a reprint of an 1885 pamphlet that first presented the tale to the world.

Morton, A. Q. *Literary Detection: How to Prove Authorship and Fraud in Literature and Documents.* New York: Scribner's, 1978. Guide to the use of "stylometric analysis" to determine authorship of texts.

Nickell, Joe. *Literary Investigation: Texts, Sources, and "Factual" Substructs of Literature and Interpretation.* Doctoral dissertation, University of Kentucky, 1987. Both a textbook and casebook approach to investigating literary conundrums, including biographical mysteries, lost texts, questioned writings, etc.

Acknowledgments

The first report of my investigation of the Beale treasure legend appeared as "DISCOVERED: The Secret of Beale's Treasure" in the *Virginia Magazine of History and Biography* (July 1982) and was subsequently reprinted as a pamphlet by the Virginia Historical Society. The present discussion—which somewhat abbreviates the explanation of the linguistic evidence and expands that of the Masonic connection—was prepared at the request of Prof. Don McDermott, editor of the journal, the *Cryptic Scholar.* I am especially grateful to Prof. Jean Pival for her invaluable assistance in this investigation.

5

Eyeless Sight

Is it possible that certain individuals have a special power enabling them to see that which is hidden from their view? If not, what is the secret to the centuries-old power known as "second sight"? How is it possible, for example, for a man to drive an automobile while securely blindfolded, as a Canadian hypnotist I investigated claimed he could do?

When I encountered this hypnotist, who used the stage name "Mr. Henry," he was playing to amused and baffled audiences on the Canadian frontier—in the town of Whitehorse, Yukon Territory. This was in the fall of 1976 when I was finishing a stint as a "stringer" for the *Yukon News.*

I had, in fact, been the correspondent from Dawson City, scene of the historic Klondike gold rush, located some three hundred miles farther to the north. There I covered the local news, including such events as a "fisherman's war" and the tragic arson of the gold-rush-era landmark, the Bonanza Hotel. But I also did the occasional feature piece. (Readers of our *Secrets of the Supernatural* will recall my tests of some "psychic prospectors"—or dowsers for gold—that resulted in one such feature.)

Mr. Henry would become the subject of my last feature article for the newspaper. My exodus from the North took me through White-horse, home of the *News,* where I was besieged by a reporter. Since Mr. Henry had just announced to the press his intentions of driving a car while blindfolded, the reporter wanted to know: "Could someone actually do this?"

I nodded solemnly.

"You mean it's not just a stunt?" the reporter asked. As he explained, Mr. Henry had alleged that his hypnotic training had heightened his psychic powers.

"Well," I replied, "I'm familiar with it as a magician's trick." I explained that it is just one of many conjuring feats known under the general heading of "second sight"—the supposed power of discerning that which is not visible, which dates back many centuries.

In the sixteenth century, for example, Reginald Scot explained how a trickster could use a confederate, or accomplice, to receive secret information. "By this means," he wrote in his classic treatise, *The Discoverie of Witchcraft* (1564), "If you have aine invention [that is, any inventiveness] you may seem to doo a hundreth miracles, and to discover the secrets of a mans thoughts or words spoken a far off."[1]

Just such feats were being performed in 1831 by the "Double-sighted Phenomenon," an eight-year-old Scottish lad named Louis Gordon M'Kean. Blindfolded and facing away from the audience, the kilted youth readily identified coins, watches, snuffboxes, and similar objects. And he could repeat what others had spoken, even though they whispered the words at a distance of a hundred yards.[2]

The following decade saw similar performances by an English woman known only as the Mysterious Lady. She performed at the Egyptian Hall in Picadilly in 1845[3] and also toured New England,[4] where she apparently caught the eye of Nathaniel Hawthorne. (He portrayed such a clairvoyant, named the Veiled Lady, in his novel, *The Blithedale Romance,* published in 1850.)[5]

Described as an "extraordinary individual" who had "excited so much interest and astonishment in New York," the Mysterious Lady performed at the Washington Hall in Philadelphia, where her advertisement stated:

> By the exertion of a faculty hitherto unknown, this lady is enabled to perform apparent impossibilities. She will describe minutely objects which are placed in such a situation as to render it wholly out of her power to see any portion of them. Repeat sentences which have been uttered in her absence, and perform many other paradoxical feats of mind. Justice cannot be done in description; suffice to say, it is the first exhibition of its kind ever seen in America, and independent of its novelty, is at once interesting, surprising and instructive.[6]

A contemporary of the Mysterious Lady, Scotland's John Henry Anderson, the Wizard of the North, had the audacity to proclaim himself the sole possessor of the miraculous power of second viewing. In his stage act he offered a mother-of-pearl case into which several ladies and gentlemen were invited to place objects, together with a piece of folded paper upon which one of them had written a brief message.

Although a member of the audience retained the box, the Wizard nevertheless read the secret writing. According to Edwin A. Dawes, in his *The Great Illusionists*:

> The feat was then taken from the realm of the apparent psychic to that of conjuring by producing the piece of paper bearing the message from an egg and commanding each article to fly from the box into a locked case held by another member of the audience at the opposite side of the theatre. Anderson would entreat the spectators to put as varied articles as possible into the box and not to restrict themselves to the usual rings, coins, and handkerchiefs so that he would have the fullest opportunity to demonstrate his remarkable powers of Second Sight.[7]

Anderson's daughters later assisted in his act, and it was Louise who allowed herself to be blindfolded and to pose as the Second-Sighted

Sybil or the Retro-reminiscent Mnemosyne. Anderson would leave the
stage for this routine, going into the audience to select the objects for
remote viewing. A bit of the duo's verbal exchange has been preserved:

> "Now darling, can you tell me what I am holding in my hand?"
>
> "Yes, dear papa, a watch chain."
>
> "You are quite right, love; it *is* a watch chain. And now, darling,
> can you tell me whether it is made of silver or gold?"
>
> "I cannot see very clearly, but I think, dear papa, it must be made
> of silver."
>
> "Yes, my dear, you are right, [to one of the audience] it is made
> of silver. Thank you. And now, angel, tell me—is it a gentleman's
> chain or a lady's?"
>
> "A gentleman's chain, dear papa" [and so on].[8]

From even this brief passage it can be seen how information can
easily be passed from questioner to respondent. All that is required
is a prearranged code in the form of a series of questions paired with
several basic categories of information. For example, "What is this?"
could denote timepieces; "Can you identify this?" might indicate money;
and so on. A similar sublist of responses could further particularize
the article: thus, "Correct!" might represent a gold pocket watch; "Right!"
an ordinary wrist watch; and "Good!" some unusual timepiece. Magician
Will Dexter gives a more complete description of a second-sight routine
in his *This Is Magic* (1958).[9]

Occasionally, though, something could go wrong, as when Dexter
was performing second sight with a friend, Tom Osterreicher, at an
after-dinner entertainment. Explains Dexter:

> Osterreicher successfully identified cigarette lighters, stamp tweezers,
> foreign coins and the usual assorted junk that we'd been accustomed
> to having thrust at us. Then came a pause.
>
> Some villain had handed me a false moustache.
>
> The nearest thing I could code was "Comb."
>
> Osterreicher said it was a comb.

I hurried on to the next victim. He was easy. Another cigarette lighter.

And on to the next. The same false moustache had been passed along the row.

We had that false moustache offered to us nine times. By the end of the performance we were both somewhat bemused.

And that, friends, is how the curtain was rung down on the Great Dexter's Unparalleled Demonstration of Second Sight.

Well—what would *you* have done?[10]

However, to thwart skeptics who might have guessed the secret, some performers utilized a method of second sight in which not a single word was uttered. Such a version was employed in 1848 by the Great French conjurer Robert-Houdin (from whom young Ehrich Weiss would later derive the name Houdini). He performed his *"La Second Vue"* (i.e., second sight) with his twelve-year-old son, Emile. The boy's eyes were bandaged and his father merely rang a bell to signal when an object was being held up for identification. One way of accomplishing this trick is by substituting a "silent code" for the verbal one. As Dexter explains:

Broadly, the silent code in this form depends on the performer in the audience signaling to the performer on the stage by a sort of semaphore system. Not so energetic, perhaps, as the semaphore you may have learned as a Boy Scout, but still a semaphore system.

A turn of the head to the left may mean "Black." To the right, "White." Left arm hanging straight down could be "Yes." Right arm straight down—"No." If you imagine, say, four head movements, four movements with each arm, four different stances, and four different methods of turning the body, you'll realize that these can convey twenty signals. Combine head, arm, stance and turning movements, and you have an enormously extended system of signaling.[11]

Naturally, such a "semaphore" system is predicated on the pretend clairvoyant's ability to see while blindfolded, although there are other means of signaling that do not depend on sight.

One of the simplest of these was employed by the great magician, Robert Heller. While his lady assistant, Haidee, lounged voluptuously and mysteriously on a sofa, Heller went among the audience to receive the proffered objects.[12]

The recumbent Haidee's divinatory powers, however, were as phoney as they were accurate. Her pose, with her head against the sofa's armrest, enabled her to hear the barely audible buzz signals sent via electric telegraph by backstage assistants.

Still another clever method requires neither sight nor signal of any kind! As Henry Hay explains in *Cyclopedia of Magic* (1949):

> The secret is that the performer and medium memorize a list of common articles sure to be found in any audience, and the performer then rushes around touching these objects *in the memorized order.* Some spoken signal is arranged to warn the medium to skip one item in case the performer cannot conveniently find it where he is.[13]

Still, being able to see while apparently securely blindfolded is a magician's secret employed by many who lay claim to mysterious powers. One such alleged power is known variously as dermo-optical perception, paroptic vision, skin vision, or simply eyeless sight. Supposedly, this involves reading printed matter by means of the fingertips, divining colors by holding objects to the cheek, or similar demonstrations.

The reputed phenomenon has appeared in various guises over the centuries, being associated, for example, with mesmerism in the 1840s. Experimental work in both the United States and the Soviet Union in the 1960s sparked new interest in eyeless sight.

For example, in 1962 a Soviet newspaper reported that Rosa Kuleshova, a twenty-two-year-old epileptic patient, could read with her middle finger—even if the print were placed under glass or cellophane. She could also accurately describe magazine pictures. Before long, other Soviet women had discovered (such is the power of suggestion!) that they also possessed this miraculous gift. Ninel Kulagina, a housewife in Leningrad, was not only able to read while blindfolded but could also propel small objects across a table, apparently by mere concentration.[14]

In the United States, *Life* magazine carried accounts of the Russian marvels in its issue of June 12, 1964. Years earlier, in its April 19, 1937, issue, *Life* had already featured the phenomenon of dermo-optical perception. At that time it was being demonstrated by a thirteen-year-old California lad named Pat Marquis, "the boy with the x-ray eyes."

Alas, each of the various x-ray wonders was soon discredited. Pat Marquis was tested by ESP (extrasensory perception) pioneer J. B. Rhine and caught peeking down his nose. When the Soviet marvels were tested in ways that did not allow them to benefit from peeking, the remarkable phenomenon ceased. Mrs. Kulagina, for example, was the subject of "alternate experiments" wherein peeking was either restricted or permitted. Her failures and successes tallied accordingly, and the scientists conducting the tests concluded: "Thus the careful checking fully exposed the sensational 'miracle.' There were no miracles whatever. There was ordinary hoax."

As magicians know, it is virtually impossible to prevent a determined trickster from peeking, since there are numerous means of making it possible. One ten-year-old Soviet girl took advantage of her turned-up nose, which helped her to circumvent a pair of opaque goggles. Many circus entertainers, such as high-wire walkers, jugglers, knife throwers, and archers, have long employed trick blindfolds, made for example by carefully scraping the cloth on the side that covers the eyes.[15]

Magic supply houses sell special blindfolds that are opaque to those examining them but translucent when donned by persons in the know. Magicians even know how to surreptitiously place a single pinhole in an ordinary blindfold that has just been inspected, thus providing ample viewing for almost any feat.

But what of a performer whose ability to perceive is limited neither by blindfolding nor shielding by solid metal? Such a "phenomenal mystifier"—as the Great Houdini called him—was Joaquin Maria Argamasilla, the Spaniard with X-ray Eyes. He could tell time from a watch whose case was snapped shut or read a calling card or message locked in a box.

Houdini investigated the Spaniard in 1924. Noting first that Argamasilla used a simple blindfold and was obviously peeking, Houdini maneuvered into a position behind the mystifier that enabled him to peer over Argamasilla's shoulder. Houdini discovered that, upon receiving a watch, the Spaniard opened it a trifle under cover of a sweeping motion, and that the lid of the padlocked box allowed a corner to be raised slightly to permit a brief glimpse of the contents. Houdini offered a test by supplying two boxes, neither of which could be opened even slightly. He later wrote, "Argamasilla failed by refusal to make a test in both instances."[16]

As to the "blindfold drive" stunt that the Canadian hypnotist proposed to perform, it too had a long and colorful history (fig. 5-7). The noted "thought reader" Washington Irving Bishop (1856–1889) performed it with a horse-drawn carriage in the late 1880s. Bishop astonished Manhattan reporters by tying on a blindfold and setting off at a gallop along a busy thoroughfare. Only once, apparently, in Milwaukee, did he crash into a tree. He claimed to have been distracted by his wife's winning her divorce suit, but he regained his composure, retook the reins, and completed his sensational demonstration.

Bishop's blindfold carriage drive has seen many imitators. It was duplicated by C. A. George Newmann—Newmann the Great—of Minneapolis. The late Milbourne Christopher, former head of the Occult Investigation Committee of the Society of American Magicians, once bicycled in Havana wearing both a blindfold and a hood. Christopher tells of magicians driving automobiles, "not only blindfolded, but with inverted metal buckets over their heads." And he once wrote, as a "word of caution to future investigators," that "hundreds of diabolically clever blindfold methods have been devised."[17]

Some performers have wads of dough placed over the eyes, followed by yards of surgical bandage and several towels. Others cover each eye with a half-dollar held in place with adhesive tape, and follow with a blindfold and then a cloth sack tied at the neck. Kuda Bux, the Kashmir conjurer, used the former method and still accurately fired a rifle at targets on the opposite side of the stage.[18]

Laymen observing such feats often come up with imaginative theories to explain them. A British performer—only one in a long line of claimants to the title, the Man with the X-ray Eyes—prompted several unique guesses when he drove a car around a farmyard. One observer opined that the alleged visionary had "fiber-optics up his nose," another that he possessed "supersensitive hearing which detected the sound of squeaking mice hidden in straw bales."[19]

However, just like the simple methods that permit one to circumvent a common blindfold, the more elaborate methods that involve multiple wrappings, hoods, etc., can easily be thwarted—as I demonstrate in the accompanying photos. (The secret, or rather som? of the secrets, of the blindfold drive and similar feats are given in Henry Hay's *Cyclopedia of Magic.*)[20]

Now, to return to the Canadian hypnotist, the Hawaiian-born Mr. Henry who was performing at a nightclub in Whitehorse, Yukon Territory: his announced blindfold drive was still days away and I would not be in town for the event. Therefore I developed a strategy that began with my attending Mr. Henry's nightclub act.

As an opening effect in the act, the hypnotist asked a spectator to tear five pages from a small pocket notebook and to satisfy himself that they were "not marked in any way." One page was then held before the eyes of his allegedly hypnotized assistant, Teo, who was instructed to "see" her own picture on the page. The spectator now placed that sheet among the remaining ones, while remembering its position. Shown the papers one at a time, Teo selected the correct one.

But how could she fail? It is a simple matter to perform such a feat. Although it is described in an old book on hypnotism as an example of "subconscious perception," it can more easily be performed as a conscious stunt, as I demonstrated the next day at lunch to a newspaper staffer. One simply memorizes some tiny flaw in the paper or the torn edge, sufficient to distinguish it from the other sheets.[21]

Next, Teo was instructed to stiffen her body, and she was placed, planklike, between two chairs, supported only by her shoulders and ankles. However, as the popular TV mentalist Kreskin has demonstrated, this is a stunt that does not depend on "hypnotism."

The remainder of the act consisted of inviting volunteer subjects on stage, with a request that disbelievers not participate since, Mr. Henry explained, they would be wasting their time and his. Thus, those anxious (or primed, as it were) to experience "going under"—along with the usual "ham" or two—were those selected. It is an accepted truth in stage hypnotism circles that a predictable few will simply play along— either because they enjoy being the center of attention or because they wish to help the nice hypnotist, or both. Some of these may be good actors, while others may appear to overreact. But there's the catch: there is no easy way of knowing to what extent the person is "hypnotized."[22]

From what I had observed, it seemed unlikely that Mr. Henry's announced blindfold drive would be more than another bit of showmanship. Since I could not remain for the demonstration, I decided on a twofold approach: First I published an article describing not the secret of the blindfold drive trick, but its history, together with a mention of *where* the secret could be found (i.e., in Hay's *Cyclopedia of Magic*). Second, unknown to Mr. Henry I left secret instructions with a reporter so that—should the hypnotist attempt to follow through on the proposed drive—someone was there who knew how to thwart all but a *genuine* practitioner of eyeless vision.

I then left town. After a brief reply to the press that he really *was* a hypnotist,[23] so did the performer and his assistant.

Notes

1. Reginald Scot, *The Discoverie of Witchcraft* (1564; reprinted from an English edition of 1930, New York: Dover, 1972), 191.

2. Milbourne Christopher, *ESP, Seers & Psychics: What the Occult Really Is* (New York: Thomas Y. Crowell, 1970), 11.

3. Edwin A. Dawes, *The Great Illusionists* (Secaucus, N.J.: Chartwell Books, 1979), 147.

4. Milbourne Christopher, *Panorama of Magic* (New York: Dover, 1962), 63.

5. See chapter 9 of Joe Nickell, *Ambrose Bierce Is Missing and Other Historical Mysteries* (Lexington: University Press of Kentucky, 1991).

6. Christopher, *Panorama,* 63.

7. Dawes, *Great Illusionists,* 110.

8. Quoted in ibid., 111.

9. See Will Dexter, "Is It Second Sight?" chap. 14 of *This Is Magic* (New York: Bell, 1958), 187–204.

10. Ibid., 194.

11. Ibid., 196–97.

12. Ibid., 195–96.

13. Henry Hay, ed., *Cyclopedia of Magic* (Philadelphia: David McKay, 1949), 314.

14. Milbourne Christopher, *Mediums, Mystics & the Occult* (New York: Thomas Y. Crowell, 1975), 77–86.

15. Ibid., 81–86; Martin Gardner, *Science: Good, Bad and Bogus* (Buffalo, N.Y.: Prometheus Books, 1987), 63–73.

16. Walter B. Gibson and Morriss N. Young, eds., *Houdini on Magic* (New York: Dover, 1953), 248–57.

17. Christopher, *Mediums,* 101–102.

18. Ibid.

19. Mick Brown, "Happiness Is a Secret Stored up Your Sleeve," London *Sunday Times,* Oct. 2, 1988.

20. Hay, *Cyclopedia of Magic,* 27–29.

21. George H. Estabrooks, *Hypnotism* (1943; rev. ed., New York: E. P. Dutton, 1957), cited in Vincent Gaddis, *Invisible Horizons: True Mysteries of the Sea* (New York: Chilton, 1965), 2.

22. Joe Nickell, "The Authenticity of Mr. Henry," *Yukon News,* Sept. 22, 1976. For a discussion of what hypnotism is and is not, see Robert A. Baker, *They Call It Hypnosis* (Buffalo, N.Y.: Prometheus Books, 1990).

23. Editor's note to my *News* feature; see above citation.

Select Bibliography

Christopher, Milbourne. *Mediums, Mystics & the Occult.* New York: Thomas Y. Crowell, 1975: 77–86. An exposé of claims of the paranormal, including "eyeless sight."

Dexter, Will. *This is Magic.* New York: Bell, 1958: 187–204. Wide-ranging presentation of the history and secrets of stage magic.

Hay, Henry, ed. *Cyclopedia of Magic.* Philadelphia: David McKay, 1949. A magicians' text that explains many conjuring secrets, including those involving blindfold feats.

Nickell, Joe. "The Authenticity of Mr. Henry." *Yukon News,* September 22, 1976. Feature article on a would-be practitioner of the "blindfold drive."

Acknowledgments

I am grateful to the *Yukon News* for permitting me to investigate, write, and publish such features as the rather brief one that provided the nucleus of this chapter. I am also grateful to Tom House, photoarchivist at the University of Kentucky, for locating the photograph of Fayssoux the Hypnotist that accompanies this chapter.

6

The Crashed-Saucer Documents
(Investigated with John F. Fischer)

I am glad of all details, . . . whether they seem to you to be relevant or not.
    —Sherlock Holmes, "The Adventure of the Copper Beeches"

Background

Whether it was an extraterrestrial craft or an ordinary balloon-carried weather device, it appears to have been swept in by the wave of UFO (unidentified flying object) reports that began on June 24, 1947, with pilot Kenneth Arnold's fortuitous sighting.[1] And now, alleged government documents purport to reveal the "Ultimate Secret": how a crashed saucer and its little humanoid occupants were recovered and hidden away at a secret government installation—all part of something called

Operation Majestic-12 (MJ-12), after the top-secret panel of a dozen scientists, military officers, and intelligence officials who allegedly comprised it.

Whatever the object was, it crashed, about the beginning of July, on a ranch near Corona, New Mexico. Although a young, public-information officer at nearby Roswell Army Air Base issued a press release stating that a "flying disc" had finally been retrieved,[2] he was soon reprimanded and the object subsequently identified as a "Rawin target." (That was a radar target formed of foiled paper fastened to a balsa frame and carried aloft by balloons.)[3] Nevertheless, rumor would soon claim that some half-dozen "humanoid creatures" had been recovered, one possibly alive,[4] and that they were hidden away at a government facility: possibly the (nonexistent) "Hangar 18" at Wright Patterson Air Force Base,[5] or even CIA headquarters at Langley, Virginia.[6]

The years brought other "crash/retrieval" stories—ranging from outright hoaxes (like that attending Frank Scully's 1950 book, *Behind the Flying Saucers*),[7] to the dubious accounts of anonymous informants (like the proliferating tales collected by Leonard Stringfield).[8] There was even a brief revival of the 1897 Aurora, Texas, crashed "airship" story (another hoax, albeit one that has been compounded over the years).[9]

Then, in 1987, came documentary evidence that proved—*if* the documents were genuine—that the "Roswell incident" was not just an absurd mistake but instead UFOlogy's "most crucial case of all time."[10] The purportedly "top secret" documents did appear under very stange circumstances. They were released by a trio of UFO researchers: William L. Moore, Jr., and two associates, Stanton T. Friedman and Jaime Shandera. Because of their crucial involvement in this important case, it will be useful to take a brief look at each.

William L[eonard]. Moore, Jr., a self-described political independent who lives in Los Angeles, was born October 31, 1943, in Sewickley, Pennsylvania, son of a steelworker and an "archivist/historian." He received an A.B. degree in 1965 and later (1968–72) attended Duquesne University without, however, receiving a further degree. He taught French and Russian in Pennsylvania public schools and English and French in high schools (1966–79) before becoming a "full-time writer and lecturer."[11] Moore tried his hand at creative writing with a couple of one-act dramas and wrote two sensationalistic books that relied heavily on shadowy sources to "expose" alleged government cover-ups: *The Philadelphia Experiment* (1979)[12] and (with Charles Berlitz) *The Roswell Incident* (1980).[13]

The former was panned by the *Washington Post*,[14] and investigative writer Paul Begg labeled the "experiment" a hoax, hinting that one source—a photocopied newspaper clipping "received by Berlitz and Moore from an anonymous source"—may have been forged.[15] Of *The Roswell Incident,* Moore later wrote: "Stan Friedman and I did the bulk of the research for the book. Berlitz was largely responsible for creating the text and format. . . . If, however, there is any blame to be taken for the disgraceful hodgepodge of fact and fiction to be found in *The Roswell Incident,* then I am willing to accept it."[16]

Since 1984 Moore has operated (with himself as president) something called the Fair-Witness Project, the avowed purpose of which is to investigate allegedly paranormal cases of "high-strange singularity."[17] He has also operated, as a business, "William L. Moore Publications & Research" (his letterhead featuring a caricature of a paste-up artist).[18] In 1989, in a speech at a UFO symposium, Moore acknowledged that he was suspected of having forged the MJ-12 documents. However, mentioning that a 1983 divorce had left him "with virtually nothing" and that he had experienced bankruptcy thereafter, he stated: "Rest assured, if I was trying to perpetrate a hoax, I would have played it for all the cash I could get a long time ago and then taken the money and run."[19]

Moore also shocked and angered many in the UFO community by alleging he had formerly acted as an unpaid government agent, providing information on several individuals as well as helping to disseminate *dis*information (ostensibly as a sort of self-appointed counter-counterintelligence operation). However, as to his reportedly once having flashed "an official identification card" linking him "with a government intelligence agency," Moore claimed: "The I.D. card thing stems from nothing more than a practical joke on my part that has simply gotten out of hand."[20]

Stanton T[erry]. Friedman, now living in Fredericton, New Brunswick, Canada, was born July 29, 1934, in Elizabeth, New Jersey, and received his B.S. degree in physics in 1955 and his M.S. in 1956 from the University of Chicago.[21] Until 1970 he worked as a nuclear physicist on classified programs for such firms as General Motors and Westinghouse. From 1970–1982 Friedman became a full-time speaker on various "controversial, scientific issues," and he served as research consultant for *The Roswell Incident*—although his name is only accorded an alphabetical position in the end-of-book acknowledgments. (But if Moore was seemingly depriving Friedman of deserved credit, the tables would soon be turned: a writing titled *UFO's: Earth's Cosmic Watergate,* which Moore listed as a work-in-progress with anticipated completion in 1981,[22] ended up as the verbatim title of a publication issued by Friedman that same year.)[23]

Since 1982 Friedman has worked as a consultant to industry on such matters as irradiated food and radon, while continuing as an active UFOlogist. According to a promotional release, he offers a "dynamic ILLUSTRATED, always UPDATED lecture 'Flying Saucers ARE Real' " that covers such topics as "saucer landings" and "abductions of earthlings by aliens."[24] In 1989, Moore described Friedman as "the scientist of the group" and defended him on a charge of "gullibility"[25] leveled by the editor of a UFO newsletter. James W. Moseley had written in his publication *Saucer Smear*:

> Friedman has recently obtained a $16,000 grant from Bruce Maccabee's Fund for UFO Research, to continue his library research on the MJ-12 matter. We would far prefer that this grant had gone to an *unbiased* observer, rather than to someone so highly committed to finding an answer that upholds the authenticity of the documents. Quite frankly, were Friedman to somehow find a "smoking gun" proving the documents are fake, we wonder if he could be trusted to reveal this information to the public & thus reveal his own gullibility of recent years![26]

Despite Moore's defense of him, Friedman reportedly became extremely angered at the implications in Moore's symposium speech,[27] with as-yet-uncertain results in regard to the pair's relationship.

Jaime H. Shandera, a Los Angeles "producer, director & researcher for 20 years,"[28] joined Moore in 1982, after having worked with him and Friedman on a UFO movie in 1980.[29] He reportedly has an "extensive background in news and documentaries."[30] However, according to a knowledgeable source, like Moore "He too has largely given up his career. . . . His financial situation is better than Moore's however, as his wife has a very good job in the TV industry."[31]

Although Shandera was a virtual unknown insofar as UFOlogy is concerned and had never published any books or papers on the subject, it was to him that the ill-fated MJ-12 papers were sent—anonymously. Shandera supposedly received them in December 1984 in the form of a roll of unprocessed 35-mm film. (It was reportedly inside a white envelope, inside a brown-paper wrapper, inside another such wrapper sealed with "official-looking brown tape on all seams." The "carefully typed" address label bore no return address.) Shandera promptly contacted Moore and the film was developed.[32]

On the film were two documents. The first was a seven-page "BRIEFING DOCUMENT: OPERATION MAJESTIC 12/ PREPARED FOR PRESIDENT-ELECT DWIGHT D. EISENHOWER," dated November 18, 1952. The second was a "MEMORANDUM FOR THE SECRETARY OF DEFENSE," dated September 24, 1947, and bearing the signature of President Truman. Both were designated "TOP SECRET/EYES ONLY."[33] If genuine, they would prove that the United States recovered a crashed saucer near Roswell in 1947, together with "four small human-like beings," and that the government also retrieved another alien vehicle that crashed near the Texas-Mexico border on December 6, 1950; the memo would prove that Truman had authorized "Operation Majestic Twelve" to handle such matters.

Then another MJ-12 document surfaced, reportedly discovered at the National Archives by Moore and Shandera in the summer of 1985. (However the copy they circulated *two years later* was marked with the release date, "1/12/87.")[34] If authentic, this document—ostensibly a carbon *copy* of a memo from Robert Cutler (special assistant to President Eishenhower) to USAF Chief of Staff General Nathan Twining, dated July 14, 1954—would verify the existence of an MJ-12 group operating at that time.

These were the primary (but not the only)[35] MJ-12 documents under contention when we became involved in the case. Our participation came with the encouragement of Jerome Clark, editor of *International UFO Reporter* (the official journal of the J. Allen Hynek Center for UFO Studies). Many other individuals and groups were involved in scrutinizing the documents—generally with a view toward debunking or defending them—but ours was to be an independent investigation.

Questioned Documents

We began our investigation by requesting from William Moore and Jaime Shandera photographic prints from the negatives they developed showing the MJ-12 documents, together with a photocopy of the front and back of the wrapper in which the film was received. Neither man troubled to reply. Stanton Friedman, however, did send us multiple-generation photocopies, stating: "I hereby certify that the enclosed Xerox copies of the Ike briefing document were made by me from prints received . . . in early August and that to the best of my knowledge they are not retouched."[36]

But Friedman was unwilling to circumvent Shandera or Moore, who, in any event, possessed the negatives; neither was Friedman willing to supply a copy of the package's postmark, which, he said, "we do not wish to reveal at this time."[37] Jerome Clark intervened at this stage to write Friedman. Clark stated that he had, for many years, known one of us (J. N.) "whose intellectual integrity I have never had reason to question," and who "has my and CUFOS' full confidence." Clark added: "All of us at CUFOS were pleased when he offered his services and I would hate to see this opportunity missed, as will happen, of course, if he has nothing to work with."[38] Nevertheless, we never received the photographs, leaving us to wonder just what Moore et al., feared could occur from our having the photos, as opposed to multiple-generation photocopies, to examine.

We had wanted the photographs for several reasons, one of which was to establish the closest possible link with the originals. Even so, without the actual papers there would be no *provenance* (i.e., history or chain of ownership) for them, and that would represent a serious obstacle to authentication. Although, as one expert states, provenance is a less crucial issue than "a thorough examination of the manuscript itself,"[39] in the case of the photographed MJ-12 documents even that was problematical.

The problem is highlighted by the fact that many notorious forgeries have involved some contrivance to mitigate the absence of the alleged "originals." For example, in the case of the spurious Beale treasure papers, the antique manuscripts had supposedly been destroyed in a fire, and only printed copies remained.[40] Again, with the bogus "Lincoln conspiracy" documents of the 1970s, the "originals" could not be examined because they were in the custody of certain "Stanton descendents" who wished to remain anonymous, so only "transcripts" were available.[41]

In the case of the filmed MJ-12 papers (the Cutler-Twining memo has its own problems), the fact that the documents were available only on film effectively prevented examination of the paper, ink, etc. It was obvious that the text and markings could easily have been supplied by old typewriters in conjunction with a cut-and-paste technique using photocopied elements from genuine documents. Indeed, this approach is one readily available to the novice forger. According to the *Journal of Forensic Sciences*:

> It has become apparent that the perpetrators of various crimes, aware of the possibility of their identification through the examinations of handwriting, typewriting, ink, or paper, have resorted to the use of photocopies in an attempt to eliminate or obscure the identifiable features of the original documents.[42]

We had also wanted the photographs to help insure that the copies we had were unaltered from the originals. (When Moore first released the documents, they had been doctored; i.e., portions had been marked out as if they had been censored—but the censorship had been done by Moore.[43] There are other ways the documents could have been altered; for example, the numerical portion of the date on the Truman memo has anomalous features[44] consistent with alteration at some stage in the document's existence.) We had also asked for contact prints of the negative so that (among other reasons) we could account for all frames and help insure that we had the full evidence as it had been received.

Because the Moore-Shandera-Friedman team had chosen to withhold crucial evidence from us, we had to make a critical decision: whether to abort our investigation, or to continue under additionally restrictive circumstances. We chose the latter. However we did advise Friedman that it would be impossible for us to authenticate the documents and that we would instead effectively be limited "to pursuing the alternate hypothesis of forgery."[45] Friedman had trouble comprehending this, and he seemed committed to defending the documents—trumpeting any credible feature and devising rationalizations for any problematical ones. To an extent this is appropriate; however, in questioned-document cases, it is not what is correct that matters nearly so much as what is wrong, since even a novice forger can be expected to get some things right. For instance, the fact that a putative George Washington letter was written on acceptably old paper would matter less than the fact that the text was written in Palmer-style penmanship; the latter would brand the document a fake. Less glaring anomalies might not be individually telling, but a number of them could represent a pattern highly indicative of forgery.

Once fully underway our investigation included making trips to both the Truman Library in Independence, Missouri, and the National Archives, consulting old government-style manuals, enlisting the aid of a linguistics expert, corresponding with UFOlogists, and much more— work that extended over a period of two years.

Even at a first reading, we saw what appeared to be a serious problem with the Truman memo. It was a glaring format error, yet one that seemed to have all but gone unrecognized. A hint of the problem comes from Friedman's berating of beleagured Philip J. Klass, arch UFO skeptic, for repeatedly calling the document a "letter." Stated Friedman:

> Klass seems to be guilty here of an intentional misrepresentation of facts by calling the memo a letter. He is able to state that authentic letters begin "My Dear Secretary" and have the full name and address of the intended recipient in the lower left hand corner of the page. And being psychic as he seems to be, he states, "But in the September 24, 1947, letter, the counterfeiter forgot to type Forrestal's name, title and address in the lower left portion of the page and used Dear Secretary Forrestal instead of Truman's typical 'My Dear Secretary.' "
>
> This is absurd. Memos—and this *was* a memo, not a letter—don't have recipients' addresses on them.[46]

Unfortunately for Friedman, neither do memos open with "Dear. . . ." That element—known as a *greeting* or *salutation*—is reserved for letters. Yet Klass acquiesced to Friedman's shrill criticism and subsequently referred to the document as a "memorandum," while correctly observing that its format differed markedly from that of authentic Truman memoranda of the same period.[47] At the very least, based on our search through countless Truman letters and memoranda as well as from Stanton Friedman's research,[48] we can say that the odds are thousands to one against such an incompetent hybrid memo/letter having emanated from Truman's office.

There were other problems with the Truman "memo" (which ostensibly served as a presidential executive order authorizing Project MJ-12). Some of these we would discover; some, others would point out. For example, soon after the MJ-12 documents surfaced, Barry Greenwood (editor of *Just Cause*) wrote:

> Page 2 of the Briefing Paper refers to the formation of MJ-12 "by special classified executive order of President Truman on 24 Septem-

ber, 1947. . . ." We have checked the Truman Library's listing of executive orders and found that no orders were issued on 9/24. Executive order numbers 9891–9896 were issued respectively on 9/15, two on 9/20, 9/23, 9/30 and 10/2/47, none even closely resembling the MJ-12 subject. There is no gap in the number sequence for these dates so none are missing. Further, the number quoted in Attachment "A" of the Briefing Paper, #092447 . . . is not an executive order number but the date of President Truman's memo, 9/24/47. Executive orders are not numbered by date but are numbered sequentially, and at the time the numbers were only four digits.[49]

Friedman's rationalization is that the document was only designated an executive order five years later (when it supposedly became an attachment to the Eisenhower briefing document), and that—in any case—we "don't have any definition of what was meant by 'special classified executive order' ";[50] therefore, he would argue, one has no basis for saying just how it might be numbered.

However, the document was undeniably being cited as an executive order (EO) by someone (Rear Admiral R. H. Hillenkoetter, if the briefing document is genuine) who should have known full well what an EO is. Besides, the document seems to function as an EO when it states, "you are hereby authorized to proceed with all due speed and caution upon your undertaking"; yet a genuine EO would necessarily explain what the undertaking *was*, and not just refer to it vaguely as "this matter."[51] Also, a genuine EO would necessarily cite the authority under which the president was acting (e.g., a specific citation, such as "By virtue of and pursuant to the authority vested in me by the provisions of . . . ," or even simply, "By virtue of the authority vested in me as President of the United States . . .").[52] In short, the document's content, like its format, seems incompatible with authenticity.

There are many other problems with this document, but we will mention only one other that we felt was quite significant—one concerning the signature. While it lacked many of the obvious indicators of forgery insofar as we could determine from our photocopy—e.g.,

Fig. 1 (*above*): historic Liberty Hall in Frankfort, Kentucky, where the "Lady in Gray" is said to tread the antique stairway and linger in an upstair's chamber known as the "Ghost Room" (photograph by Joe Nickell). Fig. 2 (*below left*): abandoned cemetery in Frankfort, Kentucky. Is it here that Mrs. Margaretta Varick—supposed to be the real-life person behind the "Lady in Gray"—is buried? (photograph by Joe Nickell). Fig. 3 (*below right*): is this "shadowy outline" of a figure that appeared in a photo of the Liberty Hall staircase a picture of the ghostly "Lady in Gray" or does it have a more mundane explanation? (photo courtesy Bill Rodgers)

71. 194. 38. 1701. 89. 76. 11. 83. 1629. 48. 94.
63. 132. 16. 111. 95. 84. 341. 975. 14. 40. 64. 27.
81. 139. 213. 63. 90. 1120. 8. 15. 3. 126. 2018. 40.
74. 758. 485. 604. 230. 436. 664. 582. 150. 251. 284.
308. 231. 124. 211. 486. 225. 401. 370. 11. 101. 305.
139. 189. 17. 33. 88. 208. 193. 145. 1. 94. 73. 416
918. 263. 28. 500. 538. 356. 117. 136. 219. 27. 176.
130. 10. 460. 25. 485. 18. 436. 65. 84. 200. 283.
118. 320. 138. 36. 416. 280 15. 71. 224. 961. 44. 16.
401. 39. 88. 61. 304. 12. 21. 24. 283. 134. 92. 63.
246. 486. 682. 7. 219. 184. 360. 780. 18. 64. 463.
474. 131. 160. 79. 73. 440. 95. 18. 64. 581. 34. 69.
128. 367. 460 17. 81. 12. 103. 820. 62. 116. 97. 103.
862. 70. 60. 1317. 471. 540. 208. 121. 890. 346. 36.
150. 59. 568. 614. 13. 120. 63. 219. 812. 2160. 1780.
99. 35. 18. 21. 136. 872. 15. 28. 170. 88. 4. 30. 44.
112. 18. 147. 436. 195. 320. 37. 122. 113. 6. 140.
8. 120. 305. 42. 58. 461. 44. 106. 301. 13. 408. 680.
93. 86. 116. 530. 82. 568. 9. 102. 38. 416. 89. 71.
216. 728. 965. 818. 2. 38. 121. 195. 14. 326. 148.
234. 18. 55. 131. 234. 361. 824. 5. 81. 623. 48. 961.
19. 26. 33. 10. 1101. 365. 92. 88. 181. 275. 346. 201.
206. 86. 36. 219. 320. 829. 840. 68. 326. 19. 48. 122.
85. 216. 284. 919. 861. 326. 985. 233. 64. 68. 232.
431. 960. 50. 29. 81. 216. 321. 603. 14. 612. 81. 360.
36. 51. 62. 194. 78. 60. 200. 314. 676. 112. 4. 28.
18. 61. 136. 247. 819. 921. 1060. 464. 895. 10. 6.
66. 119. 38. 41. 49. 602. 423. 962. 302. 294. 875.
78. 14. 23. 111. 109. 62. 31. 501. 823. 216. 280. 34.
24. 150. 1000. 162. 286. 19. 21. 17. 340. 19. 242.
31. 86. 234. 140. 607. 115. 33. 191. 67. 104. 86. 52.
88. 16. 80. 121. 67. 95. 122. 216. 548. 96. 11. 201.
77. 364. 218. 65. 667. 890. 236. 154. 211. 10. 98.
34. 119. 56. 216. 119. 71. 218. 1164. 1496. 1817. 51.
39. 210. 36. 3. 19. 540. 232. 22. 141. 617. 84. 290.
80. 46. 207. 411. 150. 29. 38. 46. 172. 85. 194. 36.
261. 543. 897. 624. 18. 212. 416. 127. 931. 19. 4. 63.
96. 12. 101. 418. 16. 140. 230. 460. 538. 19. 27.
88. 612. 1431. 90. 716. 275. 74. 83. 11. 426. 89.
72. 84. 1300. 1706. 814. 221. 132. 40. 102. 34. 858.
975. 1101. 84. 16. 79. 23. 16. 81. 122. 324. 403. 912.
227. 936. 447. 55. 86. 34. 43. 212. 107. 96. 314. 264.
1065. 323. 428. 601. 203. 124. 95. 216. 814. 2906.
654. 820. 2. 301. 112. 176. 213. 71. 87. 96. 202. 35.
10. 2. 41. 17. 84. 221. 736. 820. 214. · 11. 60. 760.

Fig. 4: Beale cipher number one, supposedly containing directions to a fabulous treasure.

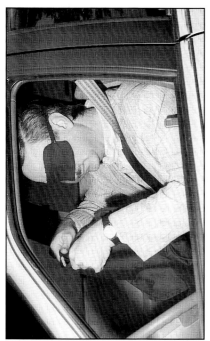

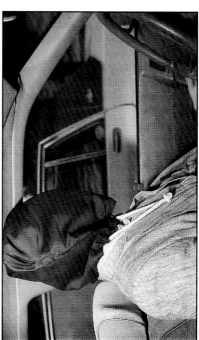

Fig. 5 (*above left*): Fayssoux the Hypnotist drove a car while blindfolded to promote his stage show at the Kentucky Theater in Lexington, Kentucky, in 1932 (photo courtesy Special Collections, University of Kentucky Libraries). Fig. 6 (*above*) and Fig. 7 (*below right*): the author dons an opaque blindfold and a cloth hood, then duplicates the celebrated "blindfold drive" feat (photographs by Robert H. van Outer).

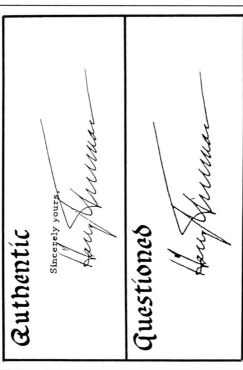

Fig. 9: Truman signature from authentic letter matches one on an "MJ-12" memo (although multiple copying has rendered the latter darker and slightly stretched). Since no two individual signatures are identical, this demonstrates that the questioned document is spurious.

Fig. 8: President Truman invariably placed his signature close to the text, as is shown in the top two examples. With the "T" as a radius, an inscribed circle cuts well into the typewriting. However, the questioned "MJ-12" example (*below*) fails this test.

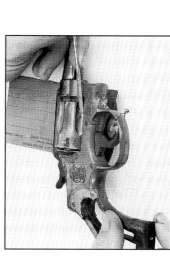

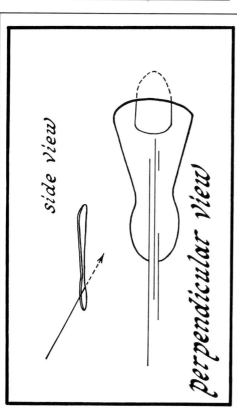

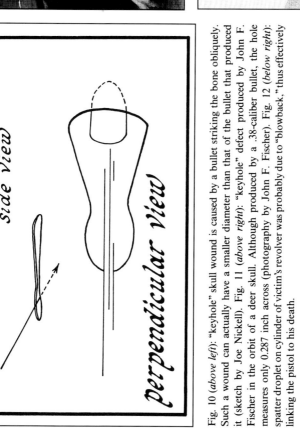

Fig. 10 (*above left*): "keyhole" skull wound is caused by a bullet striking the bone obliquely. Such a wound can actually have a smaller diameter than that of the bullet that produced it (sketch by Joe Nickell). Fig. 11 (*above right*): "keyhole" defect produced by John F. Fischer in the orbit of a deer skull. Although produced by a .38-caliber bullet, the hole measures only 0.287 inch across (photography by John F. Fischer). Fig. 12 (*below right*): spatter droplet on cylinder of victim's revolver was probably due to "blowback," thus effectively linking the pistol to his death.

Major Finds	Date	Laborers	Dawson	Teilhard	Woodward	Abbott
1. Parietal Piece	1908?	?	?			
2. Additional Pieces of Cranium	1911		X			
3. Additional Pieces of Cranium and Other Fossils and Flints	1912	P	X	X	X	
4. Jawbone Portion	1912		X		P	
5. Canine	1913		P	X	P	
6. Bone Implement	1914	P	X		X	
7. "Piltdown II" Cranial Pieces and Molar	1915		X			

X = discoverer
P = present at discovery

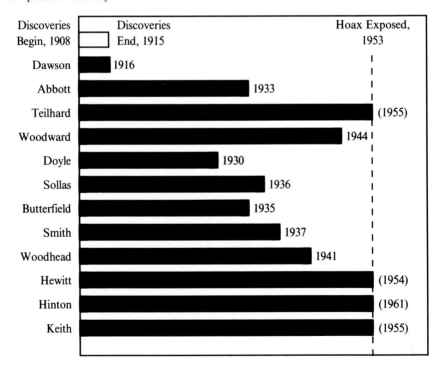

Fig. 13 (*above*): chart showing major Piltdown discoveries. Note that Dawson was the only person consistently present at the "finds." Fig. 14 (*below*): lifespans of Piltdown suspects. Note that the discoveries end with Dawson's death (computer graphic by David Davies).

Figs. 16 (*left*) and 17 (*right*): Italian Scientists' duplication of the Saint Januarius phenomenon. Congealed "blood" (*left*) liquefies (*right*) in a seemingly miraculous fashion.

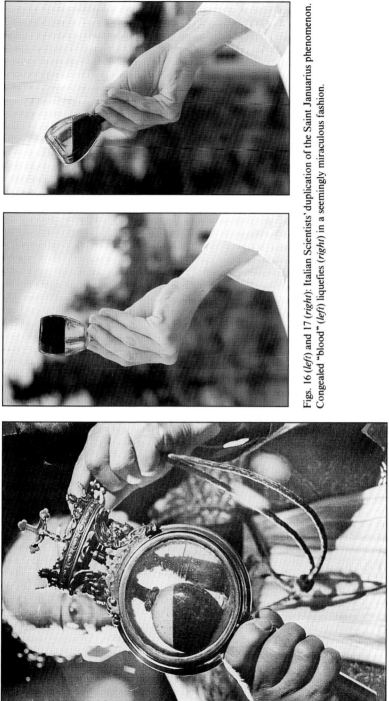

Fig. 15: the blood of Saint Januarius in its liquified state.

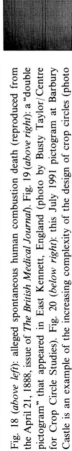

Fig. 18 (*above left*): alleged spontaneous human combustion death (reproduced from the April 21, 1888, issue of *The British Medical Journal*). Fig. 19 (*above right*): a "double pictogram" that appeared in East Kennett, England (photo by Busty Taylor/Centre for Crop Circle Studies). Fig. 20 (*below right*): this July 1991 pictogram at Barbury Castle is an example of the increasing complexity of the design of crop circles (photo by Busty Taylor/Centre for Crop Circle Studies).

tremor, retouching, etc.[53]—the document did exhibit one feature that forensic document examiners note can indicate spuriousness, namely, "Abnormal positioning of a signature with respect to the body of the writing."[54] As we learned by studying hundreds of genuine documents, President Truman habitually signed his name immediately under the body of the text, whereas the questioned Truman-Forrestal memo had the signature placed well below the text. (See fig. 8.) In combination, the apparent genuineness of the autograph and the unusual placement suggested to us that the document was a composite or paste-up type forgery made by pasting a genuine signature (such as one clipped from a photocopy) below a typed text, then recopying the whole (possibly a second time after utilizing white out to eliminate telltale margins of the cutout). That this is precisely how the memo was faked was eventually proven, but before considering that evidence let us take a brief look at the other two MJ-12 documents.

The putative Eisenhower briefing paper likewise raised many' questions. One—the pseudomilitary date format—has been the subject of much debate. Whereas the date on the cover of the document should have been written "18 November 1952," it actually contained an anomalous comma: "18 November, 1952." While Friedman has shown that such a feature, although rare, is not unknown in genuine documents of the period, he has fared less well with another date feature: the use of a zero with single-digit dates, e.g., "On 07 July, 1947." Friedman has not been able to show the use of the zero in dates of *this type*. (His citing of examples in which the representation of the date is digital— and the use of the zero therefore positional—is essentially irrelevant.)[55] We find that the two anomalous features—the comma and the zero— *when taken together* are quite distinctive. Neither we nor Friedman has been able to demonstrate the combination in a genuine U.S. government document of the period, let alone in any document produced by Hillen-koetter. (As we shall see, however, a suspect in the case has used just this distinctive date format.)

Since (unlike the brief Truman-Forrestal and Cutler-Twining memos) the Eisenhower briefing document ran to a few pages, there was a possibility of conducting a linguistics study of the text to see whether it was compatible with genuine writings of its alleged author, Hillenkoetter. Indeed, such a study had previously been commissioned by several UFO organizations, with the result that the MJ-12 document had supposedly been "validated." However, the analysis seemed flawed and quickly became the subject of controversy.[56] We therefore chose to commission a new study, and MUFON's Robert Bletchman graciously supplied a set of twenty-two Hillenkoetter exemplars that had been used as standards in the original study.

The new analysis was performed by Jean Pival, a distinguished linguistics expert who has assisted us in previous cases. Professor Pival pointed out that while she could not say conclusively whether or not the admiral wrote the briefing document, there were certainly "some puzzling deviations from the style of the other manuscripts," i.e., the exemplars, including certain "syntactical structures found sparingly or not at all in the other materials I examined." She added:

> Perhaps more significant is the inclusion of a contradictory mixing of the passive voice (elsewhere employed in relating second-hand information) and the uncharacteristic judgmental statements (found in the twenty-two Hillenkoetter memos and letters *only* in first-hand reporting). Phrases such as "highly credible military and civilian sources"; "a second object, probably of similar origin"; "the motives and ultimate intentions of these visitors remain completely unknown" probably would have been qualified in the same ways as these more characteristic ones which appear in the same document: "*what appear to be* a form of writing"; "*it is assumed that* the propulsion unit was completely destroyed"; and "*It was the tentative conclusion* of this group."

Professor Pival concluded that if Hillenkoetter did write the questioned text, "the uncharacteristic judgments could have been added by a second party." On the other hand, she said of the document, "Certainly, it could have been written by someone sophisticated enough to emulate his style."[57]

Turning finally to the Cutler-Twining memorandum allegedly discovered in the National Archives, it too raised many controversial points. Although this copy is on thin onionskin paper that could date from the appropriate time period, it apparently fails to match that actually used by Cutler at the time he served on the National Security Council. Worse, the National Archives issued a statement questioning the document's authenticity on numerous grounds, notably that it was located in a record group in which documents are filed by "a Top Secret register number," but that the questioned memo lacked such a number.[58] Moreover, although the (unsigned) copy bears the typed name of Robert Cutler, Cutler was actually *away from Washington* on the date in question. (Friedman suggests one of Cutler's two assistants—James Lay or Patrick Coyne—prepared the memo;[59] however, the Eisenhower Library counters convincingly: "one would assume that if the memorandum to Twining were genuine, Lay or Coyne would have signed it"[60]—i.e., that it would have borne one of their typed names just as did another memo issued on the same day.)[61] Even Friedman—who stubbornly defends the document against charges of fakery—concedes it may well have been "planted" at the archives (although he thinks it more likely to have been done by an "insider" than by an outside hoaxer).[62]

In the aggregate, the many anomalous and suspicious elements detected in the MJ-12 papers clearly demonstrated the documents are forgeries, but it is always desirable to find conclusive proof. The typewriting might offer such proof, but we felt our multiple-generation photocopies were unsuitable for the expert examination we had planned. (More recently, however, has come an indirect report that the Truman EO was produced on a typewriter dating from after 1947.)[63]

We saw the Truman signature as a potentially vulnerable link in the forger's chain, since we thought it was a genuine autograph affixed to a bogus document. Now, one does not sign one's name precisely the same way twice—a fact well established in the forensic literature[64]—and so part of our investigative strategy involved our attempting to find a genuine document with a signature that matched the one on the questioned Truman-Forrestal memo. One of us (J. N.), who did the searching at the Truman Library and the National Archives, was armed with a small card on which was reproduced the target (questioned) signature. This signature was compared with countless signatures, although a trained eye required only a moment or two to eliminate each from consideration. Unfortunately, although our strategy could have yielded conclusive results, we knew that it was a long-shot approach, that we were looking for a particular straw in a very large haystack.

Eventually, after we had all but abandoned our search one of us (J. N.) met Phil Klass at a conference. We had initially avoided having any contact with him, since we wished to work along independent lines, but he had learned of our investigation and—since we had also shared some information with Friedman—we did briefly discuss the case to the extent of describing our unsuccessful task. Eventually this would prove fortunate.

In time, Klass found the original—penned on an authentic Truman letter of October 1, 1947, written to Dr. Vannevar Bush—which he sent to us on a confidential basis.[65] (See fig. 9.) To his credit, he did not ask our opinion of the match; he knew (as indeed should anyone with a modicum of visuospatial skills) that he had actually discovered the signature that had been purloined by the MJ-12 forger. All he wanted from us were authoritative forensic references about the uniqueness of individual signatures, which we readily supplied.[66]

As it happens, Klass's discovery had been preempted by Stanton Friedman, with one difference: Friedman thought the correspondence of one signature to the other was proof of authenticity rather than spuriousness! In an article he published in 1987, Friedman said of the questioned Truman EO: "The signature matches that on an October 1947 letter from Truman to [Vannevar] Bush."[67] Of course, at the time, neither we nor Klass had any idea Friedman meant an identical match (even as to a distinctive, anomalous pen stroke at the top of the right-hand vertical stroke of the "H" of "Harry").

After Klass made his discovery, acting on our advice he contacted a forensic document examiner to obtain expert confirmation of his own findings. That expert was aware of another examiner's analysis that reportedly showed the Truman EO had been typed on a post-1947 typewriter. Klass immediately telephoned that examiner and the two compared notes, with the result that Klass sent the examiner the genuine Truman signature for comparison with the questioned one. Despite the fact that the latter had become slightly stretched by multiple photocopying, the examiner had no difficulty determining that the questioned signature was "a classic signature transplant," i.e., a genuine signature employed in a photocopy forgery.[68]

MJ-12 proponents, however, were having none of this. The document examiner, Klass reports—having earlier received MJ-12 material from Friedman—felt obliged to advise him of the new, negative findings and tell him "that he should just wash his hands of this." However, according to Klass, "Friedman spoke at a MUFON regional conference near St. Louis and repeated his earlier endorsement of the authenticity of the MJ-12 papers."[69]

Nor was Moore accepting defeat. Citing the slightly larger features of the MJ-12 Truman signature in comparison with the genuine Truman one, Moore grandly discounted Klass's findings. In a statement interestingly revealing of his propensity (given his publishing business) to think in terms of paste-up techniques, Moore stated: "Just as an aside, had I set out to counterfeit a signature using a Xerox, I would have cut a Harry from one signature and a Truman from another, or even tried piecing bits of several signatures together."[70]

Be that as it may, Klass is indeed correct in stating that he has uncovered the "smoking gun" in the MJ-12 forgery case. He is backed by an entire conference-room-full of forensic document examiners,[71] should our own endorsement be thought insufficient. Those who attempt to argue otherwise simply reveal their ineptitude—or worse.

The Forger

Barring either the forger's confession or a full-scale investigation by the FBI or other judicial authority prepared to obtain search warrants, conclusive identification of the MJ-12 author seems remote at this time. However, by sifting through the available evidence and considering such elements as motive, opportunity, *modus operandi,* and so forth, including linguistic and psychological factors, we have attempted to put together a composite profile of the suspect.

First of all, we are convinced the forgeries are not the work of any clandestine government agency—American or otherwise. The documents simply lack the sophistication necessary to warrant such an attribution. Instead they point unfailingly to an individual hoaxer—not only because of its typical admixture of cleverness and bungling that has characterized the solitary deceiver throughout history;[72] nor merely because it is the simplest explanation involving the fewest assumptions;[73] but also for many additional reasons.

For example, there are telltale signs of a UFO partisan at work. The most obvious example is found in the briefing document that lists the late Dr. Donald Menzel—the most militant UFO debunker of his day—among the twelve names comprising the "Majestic-12 Group." Here the hoaxer overreached, as most UFOlogists quickly realized (Stan Friedman notwithstanding).[74] Jerome Clark suggested it was a "bizarre blunder,"[75] Phil Klass, "an attempt at revenge" against Menzel.[76] Indeed, this posthumous conversion of Menzel from archskeptic to guardian of the Ultimate Secret is reminiscent of the treatment certain spiritualists have accorded Harry Houdini, the late, great crusader against spiritualist beliefs. More than one trance medium has been unable to resist pretending to conjure up the doubting magician's spirit and having him recant.[77]

Even more specifically, there are unmistakable indicators that the hoax is the work of a crashed-saucer zealot. Not only do the briefing paper's details tally with those of the "Roswell incident" as mythologized in Moore's book, but the MJ-12 papers were also clearly fabricated by someone willing to expend a considerable amount of effort in doing so. Forging the documents would have necessitated research (or access to another's research) in such repositories as the Truman Library, the National Archives, and the Library of Congress (in the Manuscript Division, in which the "smoking gun" Truman signature was discovered). Obviously, the forger was someone whose research was on a par with that of Moore, Shandera, and Friedman. Friedman and Moore had, in fact, previously gone through the very files that would soon be revealed as having provided models for the MJ-12 forgeries. (At the same time, the level of research would seem to eliminate one person who has previously been named as a suspect:[78] a former Air Force security officer, reportedly "decertified" for misconduct, named Richard C. Doty. Sources have identified Doty as William Moore's cloak-and-dagger "source," the raconteur of incredible tales whom Moore code-named "Falcon." On the TV program "UFO-Coverup?—Live," telecast October 14, 1988, a disguised "Falcon" stated that Operation MJ-12 was created "in the early fifties"—a glaring "error" that could scarcely be expected from the archival-minded MJ-12 forger.)[79]

The forger's research presupposes an intelligent individual, as does his chosen avocation since, according to an authoritative source, "Forgers approach the personality profiles of confidence men, and the latter have been shown to have above average intelligence levels."[80] Based on the profiles of many forgers, the MJ-12 forger could also be expected to be male, white, and between the ages of about twenty-seven and forty-seven at the time the documents were created. He probably comes from a middle-class, possibly "maternally dominated" home, his father perhaps having been employed in some "semi-skilled occupation" and his mother frustrated over her husband's resulting limited career abilities. Be that as it may, the culprit most likely exhibits an extroversive personality and is highly verbal and socially manipulative. He probably possesses "good organizational capacities." He may also be like others of his ilk who "rebel against all authority figures and often are cynical about general society, institutions, and mores."[81] And he can be expected to have "an exceptional amount of that type of courage which is best described as 'nerve.' "[82]

As a type of psychopath, the typical forger—and thus almost certainly our suspect—can be expected to show

> a remarkable disregard for truth. . . . During the most solemn perjuries he has no difficulty at all in looking anyone tranquilly in the eyes. Although he will lie about any matter, under any circumstances, and often for no good reason, he may, on the contrary, sometimes own up to his errors (usually when detection is certain). . . . After being caught in shameful and gross falsehoods, after repeatedly violating his most earnest pledges, he finds it easy, when another occasion arises, to speak of his *word of honor,* his *honor as a gentleman,* and he shows surprise and vexation when commitments on such a basis do not immediately settle the issue.[83]

It is well to consider, as manuscript expert Mary Benjamin observes, that forgers operate from a variety of motives, including "financial gain," "personal ambition," and "that curious form of arrested maturity which leads adults to perpetrate hoaxes."[84] It may be that in the MJ-12 forger's case, all of these are aspects of a larger motivation to silence the skeptics and rejuvenate belief among the crashed-saucer faithful. UFOlogist Dennis Stillings (of the Archaeus Project) offers an interesting suggestion in this regard (in the context of suggesting "Moore et al." may have concocted the hoax):

> These people have been committed to the hardware theory [i.e., the belief that UFOs are real, "nuts-and-bolts" extraterrestrial craft] so fanatically and for so long that they may have tired of the lack of support for what they see as obvious truth, so to save us from impending doom they have concocted a well-meaning hoax to put us on our guard. . . . This sort of thing has happened before.[85]

Because of his personality and motive, a forger who is a repeat offender (as is indicated in the MJ-12 case) will likely exhibit a characteristic *modus operandi* (or "M.O."), a method of operation that may remain relatively unchanged. That is, the typical offender is prone to "going about his task in the old familiar way, thereby leaving the inevitable indications of his identity, despite the fact that he successfully avoids leaving any other clues."[86] Thus we may hope to discover other instances of the MJ-12 forger's handiwork should there be any. They could be expected to involve forged documents, and/or their verbal equivalent, in support of a hoax exposé of an alleged government cover-up.

A more closely focused look at just the forgery aspect of the M.O. does reveal some additional clues about the person we are looking for. Earlier we mentioned verbal skills as an expected trait; the pseudo-briefing paper, allegedly written by Rear Admiral Hillenkoetter and rather cleverly imitative of his governmentese, suggests that the author is a writer who can speak through a persona. He is also able to visualize situations imaginatively. Therefore we believe we may be looking for someone who has experience in writing fiction, perhaps utilizing dialogue in stories or plays. (Of course, his may be a previously unrecognized talent; we do not suggest it is of a high order.)

His specific technology may be worthy of comment. It obviously utilized different typewriters, rubber stamps (or imitations thereof), scissors and/or a paste-up artist's knife, white correction fluid, paper, paper paste or cement, a mechanical page-numbering device (or means of simulating same), a photocopying machine, a 35-mm camera, probably a copying stand for the camera, film, envelopes, wrapping tape, etc. Of course, some or all of these could be bought or rented for the purpose, and our point in mentioning them is not so much to suggest the forger was working in an office, but that he may have had some familiarity with the rudiments of pasting up "copy," as well as using a camera, in association with publishing, and that may have suggested the particular approach to him. (We are aware that virtually anyone could type and paste up such documents and, if necessary, have someone else do the photography.)

Finally, we think the forger left something of a fingerprint on the briefing document. That is the unusual date format (e.g., "07 July, 1947," with the anomalous zero and comma). We know that this incorrect form was produced by the forger himself, who probably had used it so often that he no longer "saw" it but employed it subconsciously. (Or, for the same reason that he originally began rendering dates in that way, he may simply have never observed that it was incorrect.)

It has been suggested that this date format points to William Moore, who is known to have employed it during most of the 1980s;[87] then again, it has been suggested that the forger may have been "trying deliberately to frame Moore."[88] In regard to the latter possibility, we would suggest that anyone who might have done so would have to have had a motive commensurate with the tremendous amount of effort required, and to otherwise fit the profile we have sketched. (We do not feel that Friedman, for example, is a viable suspect.)

Laymen often suggest that no one clever enough to do *A* would be stupid enough (or careless enough) to have done *B*. Actually, anyone who will trouble to study other forgery cases (e.g., that of the "Hitler diaries" or the Mormon "Salamander" letter) will find this is not the exception but the rule. It is fortunately so for those of us who do not wish to be victimized by the smirking purloiners of truth.

Notes

1. Dr. Edward U. Condon (Scientific Director), *Final Report of the Study of Unidentified Flying Objects, Conducted by the University of Colorado Under Contract to the United States Air Force* (New York: Dutton, 1969), 11–12.

2. Roswell Army Air Base press release of July 8, 1947; published as "Roswell Statement" in *San Francisco Chronicle,* July 9, 1947. For a discussion, see Charles Berlitz and William L. Moore, *The Roswell Incident* (New York: Grosset & Dunlap, 1980), 22ff.

3. Berlitz and Moore, *Roswell Incident,* 25ff.

4. Ibid., 2.

5. Leonard Stringfield, *The UFO Crash/Retrieval Syndrome, Status Report II: New Sources, New Data* (Seguin, Tex.: Mutual UFO Network, 1980), 2ff.

6. Berlitz and Moore, *Roswell Incident,* 2.

7. Frank Scully, *Behind the Flying Saucers* (New York: Holt & Co., 1950).

8. See n. 5.

9. Jerome Clark, "UFO Crashes" Part I, *Fate,* Jan. 1988, 44–48.

10. Ibid., Part III, March 1988, 92.

11. Moore's biography in *Contemporary Authors* (Detroit: Gale Research, 1980), 93–96, 375.

12. William L. Moore, *The Philadelphia Experiment: Project Invisibility* (New York: Grosset & Dunlap, 1979).

13. Berlitz and Moore, *Roswell Incident.*

14. Henry Allen, review of *The Philadelphia Experiment, Washington Post,* March 6, 1979.

15. Paul Begg, "Immaterial Evidence," *The Unexplained II: The Mysteries of Mind, Space and Time,* reference ed. (Freeport, N.Y.: Marshall Cavendish, 1985), 1:1209.

16. William L. Moore, "Phil Klass and the Roswell Incident: The Skeptics Deceived," *International UFO Reporter,* July/August 1986, 21.

17. "Fair-witness Project," *Encyclopedia of Associations,* 23rd ed., 1989, 1:604.

18. We have one such letter dated December 7, 1987.

19. William L. Moore, "Complete Text of William L. Moore's MUFON Symposium Speech Delivered at the Aladdin Hotel, Las Vegas, Nevada, July 1, 1989," *Focus* (quarterly newsletter of Fair-Witness Project), June 30, 1989, 1–2.

20. Ibid., 8–12. See also James W. Moseley, "Glorious Rehash of MUFON's Las Vegas Convention," *Saucer Smear* 36, no. 6 (July 20, 1989): 3–4.

21. Ronald D. Story, ed., *The Encyclopedia of UFO's* (Garden City, N.Y.: Doubleday, 1980), 144–45.

22. Moore's biography in *Contemporary Authors* (n. 11), 375.

23. Stanton T. Friedman, "UFO's: Earth's Cosmic Watergate," typescript, privately printed, 1981.

24. Stanton T. Friedman, promotional flier, "Flying Saucers *ARE* Real," n.d.

25. Moore, "Complete Text . . . ," 9.

26. James W. Moseley, "Childish Feud Between Jim Moseley and Stanton Friedman," *Saucer Smear* 36, no. 5 (May 25, 1989): 4.

27. James W. Moseley, "Tidbits of Trash," *Saucer Smear* 36, no. 8 (Oct. 1, 1989): 7.

28. From Shandera's biography as given in a press release of June 11, 1987, distributed by Stanton T. Friedman.

29. Stanton T. Friedman, "MJ-12 Debunking FIASCO," *International UFO Reporter,* May/June 1988, 12.

30. Ibid.

31. James W. Moseley, "The 'MJ-12' File: Another Exclusive 'Smear' Report," *Saucer Smear* 34, no. 7 (Oct. 20, 1987): 2.

32. This information is from William L. Moore's banquet speech at the 1987 MUFON UFO conference in Washington, D.C.

33. A set of these documents accompanied Friedman's press release of June 11, 1987.

34. Ibid. See also Barry Greenwood, "The MJ-12 Fiasco," *Just Cause,* Sept. 1987, 6–7.

35. For others, see Greenwood (n. 34) and Moore (n. 19). These relate to "Project Aquarius," were released by Moore and have been revealed as fakes. (See also Barry Greenwood, "Editorial," *Just Cause,* Dec. 1987, 1.)

36. Stanton T. Friedman, letter to Joe Nickell, Oct. 9, 1987.

37. Ibid.; also letter to Joe Nickell, Nov. 19, 1987.

38. Jerome Clark, letter to Stanton T. Friedman, Nov. 19, 1987.

39. Roy L. Davids, "English Literary Autographs," in Edmund Berkeley, Jr., ed., *Autographs and Manuscripts: A Collector's Manual* (New York: Scribners, 1978), 281.

40. James B. Ward, "The Beale Papers," in P. B. Innis and Walter Dean Innis, *Gold in the Blue Ridge* (Washington and New York: Luce, 1973), 131–76; Joe Nickell, "DISCOVERED: The Secret of Beale's Treasure," *Virginia Magazine of History and Biography* 90, no. 3 (July 1982): 310–24.

41. David Balsiger and Charles E. Sellier, Jr., *The Lincoln Conspiracy* (Los Angeles: Schick Sunn Classic, 1977), 11; cf. "Caveat Emptor," editorial, *Civil War Times Illustrated,* Aug. 1977, 33–37.

42. J. E. Lile and A. R. Blair, "Classification and Identification of Photocopiers: A Progress Report," *Journal of Forensic Sciences* 21 (1976): 923.

43. James W. Moseley, "The 'Majestic 12' Documents . . . ," *Saucer Smear* 34, no. 6 (Aug. 4, 1987): 1. See also Philip J. Klass, "The MJ-12 Crashed-Saucer Documents," Part I, *Skeptical Inquirer* 12 (Winter 1987–88): 142.

44. The portion is out of alignment both horizontally and vertically, and it is reported to have been done on a different machine. See Phil Klass, "New Evidence of MJ-12 Hoax," *Skeptical Inquirer* 14 (Winter 1990): 139.

45. Joe Nickell, letter to Stanton T. Friedman, Nov. 10, 1987.

46. Stanton T. Friedman, "MJ-12: The Evidence So Far," *International UFO Reporter,* Sept./Oct. 1987, 18.

47. Philip J. Klass, "The MJ-12 Papers: Part 2," *Skeptical Inquirer* 12 (Spring 1988): 283–84.

48. In a letter of February 15, 1989, to Joe Nickell, Stanton T. Friedman stated that he was unaware of such a format in Truman correspondence, although he discounted its importance.

49. Barry Greenwood, "MJ-12 Fiasco," 4.

50. Stanton T. Friedman, letter to Joe Nickell, April 6, 1989.

51. See examples in "Executive Orders—1947," *Code of Federal Regulations, Title 3—the President, 1943–48* (Washington, D.C.: U.S. Government Printing Office, 1957).

52. Ibid., Executive Orders 9894 (Sept. 23, 1947) and 9896 (Oct. 2, 1947), 666–67.

53. Paul L. Kirk, *Crime Investigation,* 2nd ed., edited by John I. Thornton (New York: John Wiley & Sons, 1974), 472.

54. Ibid.

55. Friedman, "MJ-12 Debunking Fiasco," 13; letter (with enclosures) to Joe Nickell, June 6, 1989.

56. See Philip J. Klass, "MJ-12 Papers 'Authenticated'?" *Skeptical Inquirer* 13 (Spring 1989): 305–309.

57. Professor Jean G. Pival, letter-report to Joe Nickell, June 26, 1989.

58. Jo Ann Williamson (Chief, Military Reference Branch, Military Archives Division, National Archives), memorandum-report of July 22, 1987.

59. Friedman, "MJ-12: The Evidence So Far," 17–18.

60. Quoted in Williamson (n. 58).

61. Klass, "MJ-12 Papers; Part 2," 288.

62. Friedman, "MJ-12: The Evidence So Far," 18.

63. Klass, "New Evidence of MJ-12 Hoax," 136–38.

64. Albert S. Osborn, *Questioned Documents,* 2nd ed. (Montclair: Patterson Smith, 1978), 339–62.

65. Philip J. Klass, letter (with enclosures) to Joe Nickell, July 11, 1989.

66. Joe Nickell, letter (with enclosures) to Philip J. Klass, July 17, 1989.

67. Friedman, "MJ-12: The Evidence So Far," 16.

68. Klass, "New Evidence," 136–38.

69. Ibid., 138.

70. William L. Moore, letter (with enclosures) to Philip J. Klass (which Moore urged Klass to circulate), Sept. 23, 1989.

71. Klass, "New Evidence," 138.

72. See, for example, Curtis D. MacDougall, *Hoaxes* (New York: Dover, 1958); and Charles Hamilton, *Great Forgers and Famous Fakes* (New York: Crown, 1980).

73. For a discussion of this principle, see Elie A. Shneour, "Occam's Razor," *Skeptical Inquirer* 10 (1986): 310–13.

74. Stanton T. Friedman, "The Secret Life of Donald H. Menzel," *International UFO Reporter,* Jan./Feb. 1988, 20–24.

75. Jerome Clark, "Who was Donald Menzel?" *Fate,* Aug. 1989, 39.

76. Klass, "MJ-12 Papers: Part 2," 286.

77. See, for example, Milbourne Christopher, *Houdini: The Untold Story* (New York: Thomas Y. Crowell, 1969), 255.

78. James W. Moseley, " 'MJ-12' File," 2.

79. Klass, "New Evidence," 139; Klass, white paper ("RCD #2"), April 14, 1989.

80. E. Patrick McGuire, "Personality Profile," *The Forgers* (Bernardsville, N.J.: Padrick, 1969), 161.

81. Ibid., 159–65.

82. Charles E. O'Hara, *Fundamentals of Criminal Investigation,* 3rd ed. (Springfield, Ill.: Charles C. Thomas, 1973), 453.

83. Hervey Cleckley, *The Mask of Sanity,* 4th ed. (St. Louis: C. V. Mosby, 1964), 370–71.

84. Mary Benjamin, *Autographs* (New York: Dover, 1986), 88.

85. Dennis Stillings, letter to editor of *Saucer Smear* 34, no. 6 (Aug. 4, 1987): 6.

86. *The Modus Operandi System as an Aid in Criminal Identification* (Chicago: Institute of Applied Science, n.d.), 3–4.

87. Apparently this point was first made by British researcher Christopher Allen. See Moseley, " 'MJ-12' File," 2. See also Klass, "MJ-12 Crashed-Saucer Documents," 140. (The Moore letter we refer to in n. 18 has a date with

the two anomalous features. More recently, Moore appears to have discontinued the use.)

88. Moseley, " 'MJ-12' File," 2.

Select Bibliography

Klass, Philip J. "The MJ-12 Papers: Parts 1 and 2." *Skeptical Inquirer* 12 (Winter 1987–88): 137–46, and 12 (Spring 1988): 279–89. Evidence against the authenticity of the MJ-12 papers.

———. "New Evidence of MJ-12 Hoax." *Skeptical Inquirer* 14 (Winter 1990): 136–38. Conclusive evidence that one of the MJ-12 documents was a paste-up–type forgery.

Moore, William L., and Charles Berlitz. *The Roswell Incident.* New York: Grosset & Dunlap, 1980. Conspiracy-mongering treatment of the alleged Roswell UFO crash and purported cover-up.

Nickell, Joe. "The Hanger-18 Tales." *Common Ground,* June 9, 1984: 2–10. Treatment of crashed-saucer stories as evolving folklore.

Acknowledgments

This chapter originally appeared, in substantially the same form, as "The Crashed-saucer Forgeries" in the March/April 1990 issue of *International UFO Reporter,* and is reprinted by gracious permission of its editor, Jerome Clark.

In addition to individuals cited in the text, we are also grateful to the staffs of the Truman Library (especially Benedict K. Zobrist, director), the National Archives, and the Margaret I. King Library at the University of Kentucky for assisting in our research; to Dr. Robert A. Baker and Stuart Levine for reading the manuscript; and to Ella T. Nickell for helping in many ways.

7

The Case of the Shrinking Bullet
(Investigated with John F. Fischer)

In the afternoon of December 13, 1982, an automobile was reported
ablaze in a rural area of central Kentucky. Firefighters responding from
a nearby city discovered the burning 1974 BMW just off the blacktop,
on a graveled approach to a pasture. It was totally engulfed in fire,
but—after partially "knocking down" the flames—the firemen discovered
a body. It rested on its knees just outside the car, but the upper portion
was lying face down across the driver's side front seat. On the ground
near the victim's feet lay a .38-caliber revolver.

Police dispatched to the location secured the scene and called for
the identification division, the detective bureau, and the coroner. A police
investigation was immediately launched. Detectives learned that the white,
four-door sedan was registered to a man in another nearby city who
bought and sold thoroughbreds through a blood-stock agency operated
out of his home. During a subsequent autopsy, a dental comparison

confirmed that this "local horseman" (as the newspapers called him) was indeed the victim.[1]

On December 15, the day following the autopsy, the state's forensic anthropologist was called in, and he was able to partially reconstruct the victim's charred skull. He determined that a bullet had entered the right eye socket, producing a wound of 0.25 inch in diameter, and exited at the back of the head on the left side, leaving a wound measuring 0.45 inch. Although the entrance hole was incomplete, he insisted that the measurement was accurate "because we had greater than half the diameter of the hole."[2]

This was important because the 0.25-inch measurement was obviously compatible with a .25-caliber pistol, *not* the .38-caliber one at the scene. A bullet does not *shrink,* the anthropologist was implying. Therefore the medical examiner's office concluded that another weapon was involved and that the case was one of homicide.

The police, however, reached an entirely different conclusion about the death. They learned that the .38-caliber pistol at the scene had belonged to the victim; that he was in serious financial trouble, was depressed, and had even talked of suicide; and that he had accumulated a large sum of insurance that would pay double indemnity for accidental death or homicide, but only face value for suicide. They also determined that various claims he had made on the morning of his death—claims of being threatened and followed—could not be substantiated and were probably invented, and that he himself had actually purchased the can of kerosene with which the fire had been started, having done so just before driving to the secluded area where he was subsequently found dead.

The police dismissed the anthropologist's estimate of the bullet's caliber and rejected the homicide hypothesis. Instead, they concluded that the victim had planned his suicide to look like homicide so that his business and family would benefit from the insurance that would cover his debts.

Because of the conflicting opinions in the case, the coroner called an inquest to reach an official determination that would be recorded on the death certificate. The police presented witnesses and evidence bearing on the hypothesis of suicide (as summarized above). They also presented a video-tape reconstruction in which they showed how the victim could have started the fire in his auto, knelt or crouched outside, then fired the fatal shot—with the pistol dropping to the ground and his upper body falling forward into the flames (in just the position in which his charred corpse was found). They also presented the results of an investigation by an independent arson expert who testified that he believed the victim committed suicide. As one reason for his conclusion, the expert told jurors that the cap from the can of kerosene had been found *under* the body, indicating the car had been saturated with the accelerant before the shooting (the opposite being expected in the case of a homicide).[3]

The medical examiner and forensic anthropologist presented their findings as already briefly described. In addition to insisting that a smaller caliber gun was involved, the anthropologist expressed his personal opinion that it was "unlikely that anyone is going to have the courage to look directly down the barrel of a handgun and pull the trigger."[4]

Because, as the county attorney explained to jurors, the inquest was "a non-adversary type of hearing," the police did not cross-examine the expert nor present an expert of their own for rebuttal. Not surprisingly, therefore, the inquest resulted in a finding of homicide. One juror abstained and declined further comment. Of the five who voted for murder, two told a reporter they had been swayed primarily by the testimony concerning the bullet's caliber. As one of them stated, "I felt it was the most hard evidence we had, and it did not fit the suicide scenario."[5]

After the inquest, another independent review was commissioned by the police. This was conducted by the renowned expert in death investigations, Dr. Rudiger Breitenecker of Baltimore, who is perhaps best known for the autopsies he performed on the "Jonestown massacre" victims.

Dr. Breitenecker was "not convinced" that the defect in the fragment of bone from the area of the right eye was indeed a bullet entrance wound. Even if it were, he stated, it "represents an incomplete, fractured portion of this wound, unsuitable for definite statements as to the caliber of the bullet involved." Dr. Breitenecker also strongly doubted that a .22-caliber bullet would exit from the thick part (parietal bone) of the skull, as the anthropologist had suggested. Referring to an experiment by the anthropologist, Breitenecker stated: "The exhibit at the hearing of an old skull shot through by a .22-caliber bullet is totally misleading and irrelevant to this case. A head with skin and brain simply cannot be compared with an empty skull." In his summary, Dr. Breitenecker wrote: "The arguments concerning the caliber of the bullet involved are tenuous and not consistent with the described facts. It is my opinion that the great preponderance of the evidence supports a suicidal manner of death."[6]

Based on the findings of Dr. Breitenecker, the police decided to close the case with a determination of suicide. As they observed, a coroner's jury verdict is only advisory to the coroner and cannot mandate action by a law-enforcement agency. The action prompted an emotional response by the medical examiner who was quoted as saying the police had "sacrificed the truth."

At a forensic conference where we privately discussed the case with a police official and expressed our interest in it, we were encouraged to become involved. Subsequently, with the cooperation of the police commander who had headed the case, we launched our own independent investigation.

In addition to studying the investigative, autopsy, and laboratory reports; reviewing the testimony presented at the inquest; and examining the physical evidence, we sought to resolve the major conflicts in the case and to pursue such other avenues as we deemed appropriate.

Specifically, we analyzed with regard to their truthfulness the decedent's claims that he was being threatened and followed; conducted a review-investigation of his death and the arson of his vehicle; performed a "psychological autopsy" on the victim with the aid of a psychologist; sought to determine the caliber of the death weapon based on the "entrance" and "exit" wounds and other evidence; and performed laboratory analyses on the revolver found at the scene to determine whether there were traces of "blowback."

Alleged Threats

Quite obviously, an important issue in the case is whether or not the victim was being truthful in claiming he was receiving threatening phone calls and being followed. If the claims were true, more credence would be given to the possibility of homicide; if false, evidence is added to that indicating suicide.

At the inquest a juror inquired about the possibility of analyzing the victim's voice from a police recording of his call to them reporting the alleged threats to determine whether he had been truthful. Such voice-type "lie detector" analyses are sometimes conducted but would have been of doubtful worth in this case, even at face value, since there were no control samples of the victim's voice for comparison. Moreover, we learned that, according to one expert, "All of the reliable evidence now available shows that none of the voice stress devices is useful in detecting deception."[7] And testimony before a Senate Judiciary subcommittee held that the best-known voice-stress instrument, the Psychological Stress Evaluator (or PSE), was "no more reliable than the toss of a coin" in detecting lies.[8]

We therefore chose to forego any such voice-stress approach, instead determining to examine the victim's statements and actions concerning the alleged threats to see whether they were credible or whether, perhaps, they might reveal deception.

Briefly the facts are these. After he and his wife had risen on the morning of December 13 (the day of his death), he told her that for the past two days he had been receiving threatening phone calls. About 8:20 A.M. he called a friend to advise him of the calls, and at 8:38 A.M. he telephoned the police. He stated in part: "I've been getting about now four phone calls telling me that uh—well, 'I get you, you bastard,' and I just, you know, would like to find out what it's all about if that's possible." When asked whether he knew who might be making the calls, he replied, "I have no idea." The police communications officer advised him to call the telephone company.

When his wife returned about 8:40 A.M. (she had taken her turn at delivering her and a neighbor's children to school), he was holding the phone in his hand and told her he had received another threatening call. This time, he told her, the caller had said they were watching him. As the maid was just arriving, for privacy he went into his office and supposedly called the telephone company and also his native France to see how his sister there was doing. About this time, apparently, he wrote a note to his wife that read: "I had another phone call and I reported it to the police. So they could put a tracer on."

He left the house about 9:15 A.M., and from about 10:30 A.M. to 11:15 A.M. he visited a photo store for no apparent reason. There he told acquaintances about the alleged threats. By now he was also claiming he was being followed by a dark car, varyingly described. He next had a conversation with a bank official while waiting for his daughter at school. He made no mention of receiving threats, but when he arrived at a neighbor's home to drop off her child, he told her about the calls. He told her the callers had said, "We are watching you," and "We are following you." She looked, but saw no car that might be following him. During the twenty minutes or so that she talked with him in the driveway, she thought he appeared "upset," even somewhat "distraught." She suggested he call the police and he said he would, while neglecting to tell her he already had.

At approximately 12:20 P.M., he arrived home. He did not tell the maid of any threats or about being followed, and he appeared "sad" rather than fearful. He went into his office, supposedly to make some phone calls, and at that time wrote another note to his wife, stating that he had been "followed all morning" and that he was going to the police station, then to her father's, and then to see a man who had co-signed a $500,000 note with him. The note was overdue, and he had promised to meet with the man that afternoon. He also told one of his young daughters—who had asked about a new dog the family was getting—that he was going to pick it up. Instead, however, his body would soon be discovered in his burning vehicle.

In the days before he died, he had told no one about any threatening calls, and on the day preceding his death, when he had an opportunity to tell not only his wife but also a visiting friend, he made no mention of any threats. Yet the following morning it seems he could not tell enough people. He appears to have gone out of his way to visit the photo store to discuss the matter, and to have sought other opportunities—both by phone and in person—to tell acquaintances about the alleged threats.

He told at least two people that the caller had accused him of being "nosey" but omitted mentioning that to the police. And when he told the officer, "I can't remember doing anything to anybody," he was surely being less than candid: he must have known he had caused financial harm to several individuals. He also neglected to tell the officer he had received one of the calls just prior to phoning him, yet that is what he said in his first note.

In addition, he was obviously being untruthful with regard to all his promised errands and appointments. While he had received no phone call to change his plans that he had stated in the second note, since he posted the note as he left, he took his pistol and drove—not toward the police station as promised, but instead to the place where he died, apparently stopping along the way to purchase a can of kerosene.

Another problem related to the second note is that the black car it describes seems purely fictitious—even apart from the varying descriptions the victim gave of it. No such car was ever seen by anyone else. Significantly, no such automobile was seen in the vicinity of his BMW parked at the isolated spot. When he was first observed there at approximately 2:00 P.M. by two different witnesses, he was sitting alone in his car and no other vehicle was present.

Despite a newspaper article and police reports that mentioned unidentified vehicles near his burning auto, no one—including witnesses attracted by the smoke and converging on the scene—ever reported the presence there of any vehicle that even vaguely resembled the blue or black Oldsmobile or Chevrolet he had described.

The unidentified vehicles included a small maroon car and a black pickup truck with lights on top—both seen stopped at the blazing vehicle—and an "orangey yellow, orangey tan" pickup observed on the road about a half hour before.

We have been able to identify the black pickup as that belonging to a witness who lived nearby and who happened on the scene and briefly followed the maroon car. We also identified the other pickup as the vehicle driven by another witness who lived in the area and who observed the victim sitting alone in his car about 2:00 P.M. on the day in question.

That leaves the maroon car that cannot now be identified. However, we note that all the available evidence indicates that car did not arrive until after the fire had burned for a few minutes, and that it stopped only briefly at the burning vehicle. Its occupants were two teenagers who, according to the witness who followed them, "didn't act like they was trying to get away." We conclude that the pair were merely passers-by who had nothing whatever to do with the death. It is unlikely that the youths were even aware there was a body in the car; the witness stated he could not at that time see a body due to the smoke.[9]

That the victim was sitting alone in his car in a secluded area is in itself a very, very strong indication that his claims of being threatened and followed were false. Surely if he were indeed afraid, as he attempted to make others believe, he would not have put himself in such a vulnerable position. In actuality, his sitting alone there for approximately half an hour suggests he was contemplating his suicide and getting up the courage to follow through on his plan.

The Death and Fire

When the victim left his home for the last time, instead of driving to the police station as promised, he probably drove approximately four miles in the opposite direction to an oil company. There—on that or an earlier day—he is known to have purchased a can of kerosene, taking the trouble to tell the part-time employee who sold it to him it was to be used to keep his other car from freezing up.

Although the exact date of the purchase cannot now be determined with certainty, it was on an afternoon close to the day of his death, according to the employee. The police did examine the business's cash register tape for December 13 and found an unidentified item that had sold for the price of the fuel can, but it was impossible to prove the purchase was made on that day.

In any event, the very purchase of the fuel can and flammable liquid is suggestive because, as the police observed, there was no reason why the victim would need a new container and kerosene since he already had a supply at his home.

By approximately 2:00 P.M. on the thirteenth the victim was at the graveled pull-off spot. This was a locale known to him, according to his wife who testified at the inquest that she and her husband were familiar with the road from taking drives in the country. The BMW— which had clearly not been forced off the road[10]—was the only car there at the time. Not only was the victim sitting inside, alone, when the witnesses saw him, but he also was not slumped over and appeared normal.[11]

Some half hour or so later, the evidence suggests, he shot himself. The most likely scenario is that he doused the inside of the car—mostly the front-seat area—with kerosene, tossed in the can, then set the accelerant on fire. Unlike gasoline, which would have burst too violently into flames, the kerosene gave him several seconds to position himself and fire the shot.

He held the pistol in such a way as to cause the bullet to enter from the front (although the trajectory was still consistent with the bullet's being fired by a right-handed person). He pulled the trigger and the pistol discharged. As the pistol went to the ground, his upper body slumped forward into the seat.

He was not dead at this time since the autopsy revealed evidence of smoke inhalation including carbon monoxide in the blood. As the fire progressed and his vital signs ceased, his body became "massively incinerated."[12] Eventually the entire vehicle became engulfed in flames that "spread from the area of the driver's door back to the rear of the vehicle."[13]

In discussing the case with some interested laymen we found that many had difficulty accepting such a death as a suicide. More than one remarked that it seemed impossible for someone to "shoot himself and then set himself on fire." Of course, that is not at all what happened, and such a statement merely reveals misinformation. So does the anthropologist's statement during the inquest that for the gun to have been lying where it was, the victim would have to have "shot himself, switched hands and pitched it out the window."[14]

We suspect that some persons try to imagine themselves in the victim's situation and—since they find the thought of burning frightening—have difficulty believing anyone else could commit such an act. But persons *do* cremate themselves, including Buddhist martyrs who protested the Vietnam War. Indeed, as the authors of a treatise on suicide observe, "self-cremation" is less rare than is generally believed; they cite "nine cases of persons who chose to die in this way in recent years." As they state, "Some persons simply pour an inflammable liquid on their clothing and set a match to it. Others leap into furnaces."[15]

Spitz and Fisher, in their forensic text, *Medicolegal Investigation of Death*, detail a case of this type in which a burning auto was discovered containing the body of a man (who "had become increasingly depressed") together with a charred one-gallon fuel can.[16] In another instance, witnesses saw an Ohio college student douse himself with gasoline at a Kentucky service station, jump into his car, and burn himself up on the highway, using a lighter he had just taken away from a woman.[17]

However, according to suicide experts, "Few elect to die in this horrifying way, and the consensus is that those who do are insane, desiring to punish themselves severely."[18] And, according to Svensson and Wendel's *Techniques of Crime Scene Investigation*, "generally the suicide, immediately after starting the fire, has employed other measures to shorten his life."[19]

A person may carry out his or her suicide in quite a bizarre fashion. In a recent Kentucky case of which we are aware a man who wished to die apparently also wished to disguise the fact by creating the illusion he had disappeared. He first told his family he was going out west. Then he went to a wooded area, dug a thirty-inch-deep grave, crawled inside, pulled a door over it, and shot himself in the head with his own .357 Magnum pistol. Presumably because he realized his body might still be discovered, he left a note "indicating his despondency and his intent."[20]

It should come as no surprise that a case with atypical features might prove to have an atypical solution. Viewed as either a suicide or a murder, the case we were investigating clearly had such. If the victim killed himself, for example, there are the gunshot to the eye and the fire that statistically are unusual. Or, if he were murdered, there is the presence of his own fired revolver and his purchase of the accelerant. Those are among the unusual features for a homicide.

Psychological Autopsy

To assess the victim's psychological state relative to the possibility of suicide, we decided to conduct what is called a "psychological autopsy." This is the primary method of assessing the psychological state and personality characteristics of the possible suicide victim.[21]

The purpose of the psychological autopsy is "to reconstruct the final days and weeks of life by bringing together available observation, fact and opinion about a recently deceased person in an effort to understand the psychosocial components of death."[22] Many factors can be taken into consideration, such as the victim's personality and lifestyle, any recent failures or successes he or she might have experienced, certain mood changes, and so forth.

If suicide were indeed a credible hypothesis for this death, we should expect to find attendant factors usually associated with one's taking of one's own life. It is generally agreed that depression is a common factor, and some studies suggest that a mood change to depression may be one of the more reliable indicators.[23] Other important cues that have been noted include "financial difficulties" and "a feeling of disgrace."[24] In a study that compared male suicides with driver fatalities, it was found that the suicides were "significantly more negative, helpless, suspicious, anxious, withdrawn, nervous, bizarre, and depressed" than those in the comparison group.[25] In a social-clinical study, Kobler and Stotland argued that "the loss of purpose and hope" could generally characterize those who attempted suicide,[26] and Lester concluded "that there is some evidence that suicidal persons do lack hope, especially with regard to their social isolation and alienation."[27]

Indeed, a lack of hope does seem to characterize the victim's own response to his growing financial problems. Over several months' time his monetary troubles had grown to overwhelming proportions, and he had suffered failure after failure in the days preceding his death. Among his debts were a $500,000 note on a New Orleans bank that was several days overdue; a nearly $200,000 debt owed a local bank; large overexpenditures charged to VISA, MasterCard, and American Express—some $27,000 due American Express alone; and numerous other debts. His wife testified that at his death his estate's liabilities were approximately 1.5 million dollars, with assets of only about $400,000.[28]

His checks had bounced; he seemed unable to obtain further credit; and the "financial strain" was beginning to show, according to several persons close to him. His maintenance man said that his "moods would come and go, that sometimes he would be depressed." Two of his closest friends stated he had become "extremely upset and worried over his credibility and standing in the horse community." He had reportedly "begun to leave his phones off the hook due to the fact that various creditors were trying to contact him."[29]

His wife told police that for over a month her husband had been desperately attempting to get French money into the United States to pay some of his debts. Approximately ten or eleven days before his death he had gone to France on a financial "emergency"; he had horses to be auctioned there but none sold, and the trip was a failure.[30]

In response to such failures, he was driven to more and more desperate schemes to delay payment of his mounting debts. For example, pressed by a bank officer, he lied that his horses had sold in France for $500,000; he told a business associate a similar falsehood. Evidence of other of his financial schemes was uncovered by police investigators who found that "several horses listed in limited partnership agreements did not exist and/or liens were found on the horses and their foals." Also, among his papers was a letter—purportedly from his bank but actually a forgery—saying his assets had been frozen by the IRS; this was obviously a ruse to stall creditors. Moreover, according to informants, he was reportedly "trying to get ten people to put in $500,000.00 each for a five million dollar horse deal."[31]

In his last days, some acquaintances found him in good spirits, while others noted he seemed "tired" or "preoccupied." On the day of his death he seemed "worried" or even "distraught." And when he bade his daughters goodbye for the last time, his maid had regarded him as noticeably "sad" (as police recorded she told them before she had learned of her employer's death). At the inquest she testified he had a "different expression on his face" than usual, one that she thought indicated he might be "depressed."[32]

An apparently image-conscious man—described as "very proud," "meticulous" in his personal habits, and as evidencing concern over his social standing—he seems to have largely kept his problems to himself; "bottled up" is a common way of expressing it. For example, his wife said of his business, "He kept that to himself." And although she thought her husband's financial problems might have been large, she did not actually know. Her father—with whom he owned a bloodstock agency— was shocked to learn the magnitude of his son-in-law's debts or that he had purchased large amounts of life insurance. Likewise, business associates had little idea of the extent of his debts; instead he would speak of a "cash-flow problem" intimating that he was merely having trouble getting money transferred from France.[33]

As the pressure on him steadily mounted and as potential avenues of escape from his difficulties became closed, he apparently began to contemplate suicide. On one or two occasions he remarked to a close friend, "My God, the way things are going, sometimes I think—the pressure of this business—if it wasn't for my wife and my children, sometimes I feel like I'd blow my head off." However, he may have come to realize that in a sense he could have it both ways: he could escape from his troubles by dying and could provide for his family with the insurance money. Such scheming involving money would be consistent with some of his actions already described.

The victim's behavior on the day of his death became increasingly erratic. For example, he had neglected to shave—a fact that, given his "meticulous" personal habits, was thought noteworthy by several persons who spoke with him before his death. One such person described him as unkempt and preoccupied and said his "conversation did not sound very intelligent."[34] Also that day he began to make the wild claims about receiving threatening phone calls and being followed.

In brief, a look at the final days of his life reveals several of the factors frequently associated with suicide: financial problems and impending disgrace; anxiety, withdrawal, and depression; and a general lack of hope. Indeed, the persistency of his failures would seem to have resulted in what Dr. Irving Berent terms "chronic unrelenting stress syndrome," a condition of severe anxiety produced by such continual duress—what Dr. Berent refers to as an "onslaught" of trauma—as to cause "erosion of the spirit" and even suicide.[35] The victim's psychological state, together with his specific mention of the possibility of taking his own life, strongly suggests his potential for suicide, according to psychologist Michael Yocum, who assisted with this "psychological autopsy."

Study of Entrance and Exit Wounds

Virtually the entire argument for homicide in the case rests on the forensic anthropologist's insistence that the victim's .38-caliber pistol—found at the scene with one shot fired—could not possibly have caused the entrance wound in the right eye. Instead, he argued that the wound was produced by a much smaller caliber weapon—one of .22 or .25 caliber. Although the presumed entrance wound was only a semicircular defect in a fragment of bone, he felt he was able to estimate the diameter of the bullet that supposedly caused it. If he was correct, then another weapon—a weapon missing from the scene—killed the victim and therefore the death was a homicide.

After studying and rephotographing the bone fragments, we agreed with the anthropologist that the semicircular defect was indeed a bullet hole (police had speculated that it might have been caused, for example, by a spring from the car seat), and we agreed with his measurements.

However, we also concluded that the exit wound's large diameter (about 0.45 inches) and the relative thickness of the skull at that point suggested a .38 caliber rather than a .22- or .25-caliber bullet had produced the wound.

More significantly, a search of the forensic literature soon made us aware that the entrance wound is of a type known as a "keyhole defect" in which a circular or elliptical portion of the defect is at the point of entry, and a triangular or wedge-shaped portion is located away from the point of entrance.[36] Still more significantly, we learned that such a keyhole defect—which results from a bullet striking thin bone at an angle—may have its circular or elliptical portion *much smaller then the caliber of the bullet that produced it.* Boston Medical Examiner Douglas S. Dixon describes just such an instance in which a .32-caliber semiautomatic weapon produced a classic keyhole defect, the circular portion of which measured only one-quarter inch across.[37]

Because of his expertise in this area, we asked Dr. Dixon to evaluate our case. In a subsequent letter report he wrote: "I have examined the material submitted with special emphasis on Dr. Breitenecker's evaluation; I respect and admire Dr. Breitenecker and completely concur with his stated opinion." Further on he stated:

It may be valid to exclude certain caliber projectiles from consideration based on the diameter of bony defects at the entrance site. I would, however, be unwilling to do so in this case where a partial portion of the defect is recovered, and where there has been extensive heat effect. To do so with the implications evident in this case is extremely hazardous and does little credit to the subspeciality.

We had mentioned to Dr. Dixon a possible explanation for keyholing: that as it strikes the bone tangentially, the bullet's rounded nose creates the initial small hole, and a triangular portion of bone is knocked free (or shattered into fragments) ahead of it. As the main portion of the bullet passes through the now-semicircular opening, it forces open the "jaws" of the same, thus allowing the larger bullet to pass on through. (See fig. 10.) Dr. Dixon responded:

You have asked me specifically whether the entrance defect could be a "keyhole defect." The physics associated with the formation of a keyhole are complicated, and I am not a physicist. Your hypothetical explanation seems reasonable to me. Of importance in this case is the curved configuration of the orbit, making a tangential shot quite likely; many of my research "keyhole lesions" were clearly associated with a tangential impact of the skull.

He added:

Also important is the observation that many of the projectiles recovered in my cases were incomplete with shaving off of a portion of the bullet at the entrance; this would decrease the size of the bullet and perhaps explain why an entrance hole could be smaller than the initial bullet caliber.

And as to the instance (cited above) of a .32-caliber bullet leaving a one-quarter-inch defect, Dr. Dixon said: "Whatever phenomena accounted for this finding could certainly apply" in our case.[38]

In fact, one of us (J. F.) succeeded in producing a keyhole defect that measured significantly smaller in diameter than the caliber of the bullet that caused it. The pistol used was a Smith and Wesson .38-caliber revolver similar to the victim's, and it was fired into the orbit of a deer skull. The resulting entrance defect (see fig. 11) is comparable to that in the victim's right orbit and measures only about 0.287 inch across.

We therefore believe the keyhole-type appearance of the entrance wound in the deceased's right orbit, taken together with the relatively large size of the exit wound, makes it entirely possible that the .38-caliber weapon found at the scene was indeed the death weapon. This possibility led us to examine the pistol quite carefully for what is known as "blowback"—blood or other matter from the body spattering on the weapon at the time of firing—the presence of which would warrant the conclusion that the victim's pistol was in fact the one that caused his death.

Examination of Revolver for "Blowback"

As part of the original investigation, tests for "blowback" on the victim's revolver were conducted by the Kentucky State Police Laboratory. Although those tests were negative, they were only for "blood or tissue" and apparently did not include attempts to identify eye fluids (aqueous humor and vitreous humor). Also the report did not state what methods were employed.[39]

Our new analyses consisted of macroscopic and microscopic examination, ultraviolet and infrared inspection, both laser-induced fluorescence and laser-induced infrared fluorescence examinations, laser/chemical tests, and conventional presumptive chemical tests.

Close visual inspection showed—in addition to numerous large, stained, and blackened areas—several small spatter droplets that were potentially due to blowback. They measured approximately 1mm. or smaller. It seems unlikely the droplets spattered on the gun after it was hot, since water and other nonviscous liquids tend to "dance" on the surface; also, more viscous and proteinaceous liquids tend to stick and bead rather than form the classic "tadpole" shape or "exclamation-point" appearance of spatter droplets found on the revolver.

One of the most prominent of such spatters was discovered on the right side of the cylinder (fig. 12), and since the pistol was found lying on its right side at the scene, it would seem unlikely that that particular droplet occurred after the pistol fell to the ground.

Following inspection with a stereo microscope, we removed minute samples for further examination. At this time particulate matter was also collected from the inside of the barrel. All of these samples were subjected to polarized-light microscopy and a series of microchemical analyses, including a catalytic test for blood, and further tests for amino acids (which might have survived thermal decomposition of any biological fluid) and glucose (a constituent of vitreous humor that would not otherwise be expected to be found on a firearm). All these tests were negative, but the small amount of available samples and the extreme heat to which the weapon was subjected could well have been limiting factors.

Visual examination utilizing both short- and long-wave ultraviolet light likewise revealed nothing significant. Infrared examination using a high-resolution, extended infrared video system was also unproductive.

Our next examination utilized an 8-watt argon-ion laser with tunable optics. This technique was chosen because of a particular property of blood that the laser is capable of exploiting. When blood is subjected to increasing heat, and at the same time is excited by the 514-mm. wavelength of laser light, it forms fluorescent compounds that subsequently decompose to nonfluorescent compounds. Therefore, if the stains on the pistol were actually blood and had not reached the point of nonfluorescence, an observable bright orange luminescence would be detected. Unfortunately, this test also proved negative (although other fluorescences were observed that were characteristic of gunpowder residue and resinous sealant from the burned-off pistol grips).

However, we were able to extend this methodology by combining the laser with the infrared video system, thus making possible the detection of fluorescence not otherwise observable. Areas of infrared fluorescence were thereby observed, e.g., on—as well as just in front of—the trigger guard. This alone does not prove the presence of blood, but with the addition of certain reagents we obtained laser-induced chemolumines-cence that was characteristic of blood. This was observed in the pre-viously mentioned areas as well as on the left side of the cylinder and on the side of the barrel at the muzzle end. The results of this test, in conjunction with the laser-induced infrared fluorescence, do provide an indication—although not a positive identification—of blood.

While the stains could not be further characterized chemically, their physical appearance was so distinctive that we felt it necessary to consult someone specifically trained in blood-pattern interpretation. Therefore we consulted with nationally recognized bloodstain-pattern analyst Judy Bunker. She told us:

> In instances where a gun is fired producing an injury, blood is often found to spatter back toward the weapon at the moment the projectile impacts the body, particularly the head. Due to the force associated with this type of impact, the blood is broken apart into tiny droplets and is deposited on persons or objects located nearby. If a weapon is placed within inches of the injury site, small mist-like droplets of blood are often seen on the barrel, cylinder, and trigger guard, as well as other surfaces. The location of blood staining would depend on the position of the weapon and the hand holding the weapon at the moment of bloodshed.

In presenting the weapon to her, we informed her it was suspected of being used in a shooting, and that the deterioration of the weapon precluded the opportunity to document bloodstains. We asked her to consider whether the presence of questionable stains on the weapon might be associated with blowback. Following a careful examination of the revolver, she stated: "The locations of the stains and their size and shape are compatible with spatter produced by a gunshot wound."[40]

This evidence that the spatter droplets on the pistol are probably blowback, added to the previous evidence that a .38-caliber weapon fired the fatal shot, convincingly links the victim's pistol to his death.

That it was wielded by his own hand is, as we have seen, strongly argued by several elements, not the least of which are his proliferating but unconvincing and conflicting claims about being threatened and followed, together with his failure to go to the police department or to meet with other persons as supposedly planned. These suspicious elements are underscored by his driving instead to an isolated spot and sitting alone in his car for a time (as observed by two different witnesses). That he himself purchased the kerosene used for the fire is a very, very strong indication that he planned his own disguised suicide.

A "psychological autopsy" on the victim revealed several factors often associated with suicide: financial problems and impending disgrace, withdrawal and depression, and a general lack of hope. Indeed, he seems to have experienced what is known as "chronic unrelenting stress syndrome." His psychological state and the fact that he specifically mentioned the possibility of taking his own life are strong indicators of his potential for suicide, according to a psychologist who assisted us in our investigation.

Finally, there is the question of motive. Given that he had purchased a large amount of life insurance that could pay double indemnity for accidental death or homicide, a suicide disguised as a homicide might allow him to escape from his unbearable situation, and the resulting insurance money would protect his family from financial ruin.

Certainly the death was a strange one. Yet the preponderance of direct, real, and circumstantial evidence, including that yielded by our new investigation, strongly indicates that the victim caused his own "homicide." Despite the illusion of the "shrinking bullet," we have indeed identified what quite literally was the "smoking gun."

Notes

1. The identity of the deceased is being withheld out of respect for his family. Except as otherwise noted, information for this chapter is taken from

various reports and records in the police file on the case, together with newspaper articles on the related events. The chapter is abridged from our report to the police dated July 26, 1985.

2. Proceedings of a coroner's inquest held March 1 and 2, 1983.

3. Ibid. Prior to the inquest, the distinguished pathologist, Dr. Lester Adelson, Professor of Forensic Pathology at Case Western Reserve University School of Medicine, was commissioned by the police to review the various findings in the case. Unfortunately, he and his consulting physical anthropologist, Dr. C. Owen Lovejoy, could "neither confirm nor contradict the other details of the original opinions solely on the basis of our independent study."

4. Inquest proceedings.

5. Ibid.

6. Dr. Rudiger Breitenecker, letter report to police, May 9, 1983.

7. Frank Horvath, "Detecting Deception: The Promise and the Reality of Voice Stress Analysis," *Journal of Forensic Sciences* 27, no. 2 (April 1982): 340–51.

8. John A. Jenkins in an article in the *Washington Post*, Sept. 2, 1979, cited in Philip J. Klass, "Beware of the 'Truth Evaluator,' " *Skeptical Inquirer* (Summer 1980): 44–51.

9. Police reports (see n. 1) and inquest proceedings.

10. Inquest proceedings.

11. Ibid.

12. Autopsy report, no. ME-82-875 (see n. 1).

13. Independent fire investigator's report, January 17, 1983 (see n. 1).

14. Inquest proceedings.

15. Edward Robb Ellis and George N. Allen, *Traitor Within: Our Suicide Problem* (Garden City, N.Y.: Doubleday, 1961), 141.

16. Warner U. Spitz and Russell S. Fisher, *Medicolegal Investigation of Death* (Springfield, Ill.: Charles C. Thomas, 1980), 51–54.

17. "Driver Dies in Fiery Suicide on I-64," *Morehead News* (Morehead, Ky.), May 8, 1984.

18. Ellis and Allen, *Traitor Within,* 141.

19. Arne Svensson and Otto Wendel, *Techniques of Crime Scene Investigation* (New York: Elseiver, 1965), 389.

20. "Fort Thomas Man Dug Grave, Killed Himself, Police Believe," *Courier-Journal* (Louisville, Ky.), Feb. 22, 1984.

21. Seymour Perlin, *A Handbook for the Study of Suicide* (New York: Oxford University Press, 1975), 158.

22. Avery D. Weisman and Robert Kastenbaum, *The Psychological Autopsy: A Study of the Terminal Phase of Life* (New York: Behavioral Publications, 1968).

23. David Lester, *Why People Kill Themselves* (Springfield, Ill.: Charles C. Thomas, 1972), 263.

24. Eli Robbins, *The Final Months: A Study of the Lives of 134 Persons Who Committed Suicide* (New York: Oxford University Press, 1981), 415.

25. Perline, *Handbook for the Study of Suicide,* 160.

26. Arthur L. Kobler and Ezra Stotland, *The End of Hope: A Social-clinical Study of Suicide* (London: The Free Press of Glencoe, 1964), 14.

27. Lester, *Why People Kill Themselves,* 271.

28. Police files and inquest proceedings.

29. Ibid.

30. Ibid.

31. Ibid.

32. Ibid.

33. Ibid.

34. Inquest proceedings.

35. Irving Berent, *The Algebra of Suicide* (New York: Human Sciences Press, 1981).

36. D. S. Dixon, "Keyhole Lesions in Gunshot Wounds of the Skull and Direction of Fire," *Journal of Forensic Sciences* 27, no. 3 (July 1982): 555–66.

37. Ibid.

38. D. S. Dixon, letter report to Joe Nickell, Feb. 20, 1985.

39. This "Report of Crime Laboratory Examination," dated Feb. 4, 1983, is in police files.

40. Judy Bunker, personal communication to John F. Fischer and Joe Nickell, June 14, 1985.

Select Bibliography

Dixon, D. S. "Keyhole Lesions in Gunshot Wounds of the Skull and Direction of Fire." *Journal of Forensic Sciences* 27, no. 3 (July 1982): 555–66. Study of a distinctive type of bullet wound.

Spitz, Warner U., and Russell S. Fisher. *Medicolegal Investigation of Death.* Springfield, Ill.: Charles C. Thomas, 1980. Forensic textbook on investigating deaths.

Weisman, Avery D., and Robert Kastenbaum. *The Psychological Autopsy: A Study of the Terminal Phase of Life.* New York: Behavioral Publications, 1968. Treatise on attempting to understand the psychological factors that may have bearing on a person's death.

Acknowledgments

A synopsis of this case, together with the scientific findings of our experiments in producing keyhole lesions, was given in John F. Fischer and Joe Nickell, " 'Keyhole' Skull Wounds: The Problem of Bullet-caliber Determination," *Identification News,* December 1986: 8–10.

We appreciate the professional assistance of Judy Bunker, the noted blood-pattern analyst; Dr. D. S. Dixon, the Boston medical examiner; and Michael Yocum, psychologist. We are also grateful once again to Robert H. van Outer for his photographic work on our behalf.

8

The Piltdown Perpetrator
(Investigated with John F. Fischer)

Controversy over just who perpetrated "the greatest hoax in the history of science"[1]—the bold Piltdown forgery—continues, and the number of persons accused of being the culprit increases with the passing years. But has the real hoaxer been identified?

By now, the basic elements of the affair are quite familiar. In December of 1912 a major scientific discovery was announced. The long-sought-after "missing link" between man and his ancestors had been recovered from a gravel pit near Piltdown Common in Sussex by an amateur fossil collector named Charles Dawson. Although there were a few skeptics, Piltdown Man appeared to be the transitional form postulated by Charles Darwin's theory of evolution.[2]

The discovery also appealed to English pride; previous anthropological discoveries had been made in Europe and Asia. Neanderthal man had been found in Germany (1856) and Cro-Magnon in France

131

(1868). France had also been the scene of a hoax that foreshadowed the one at Piltdown. (In 1863 in a gravel pit at Moulin Quignon, near Abbeville, some flint implements were "discovered" together with an ancient human jaw. It was soon learned, however, that the relics had been artificially stained.)[3] Accepted as authentic despite the doubts of a few skeptics, Piltdown man (named *Eoanthropus dawsoni,* that is, "Dawson's Dawn Man") became the subject of countless scholarly articles and books, was enshrined in the British Museum, and won prominent display in the American Museum of Natural History's Hall of Man.

The illusion of the fossil hominid that was half human, half ape lasted for more than four decades. Then in 1953 the hoax was exposed, and the glare of suspicion fell upon Dawson. However, his chief accuser, Dr. J. S. Weiner, conceded in his *The Piltdown Forgery* (1955):

> So long as the weight of circumstantial evidence is insufficient to prove beyond all reasonable doubt that it was Dawson himself who set the deception going by "planting" the pieces of brain-case, our verdict as to the authorship must rest on suspicion and not proof. In the circumstances, can we withhold from Dawson the one alternative possibility, remote though it seems, but which we cannot altogether disprove: that he might, after all, have been implicated in a "joke," perhaps not even his own, which went too far? Would it not be fairer to one who cannot speak for himself to let it go at that?[4]

Since Weiner wrote those cautious words, seeming droves of armchair detectives have rushed to don their deerstalkers and puff away at the problem of identifying the "actual" culprit. Unfortunately these amateur sleuths have recklessly accused just about everyone connected with the affair—from respected scientists and a young priest to, somewhat ironically, the creator of Sherlock Holmes.

So what is the solution? Was Dawson an innocent victim as some would hold or, as others suggest, a co-conspirator or even sole perpetrator? Whatever our answer, it must come with the realization that the passage of time has meant the loss of much valuable evidence. For instance, most of Dawson's personal papers were destroyed in the year after his death, and many others, including the manuscript of a book that brought him charges of plagiarism, were sacrificed to World War II salvage efforts.[5] And there are other lamentable effects of time.

For example, the story of how the first bone fragment was found about 1908 is told in so many versions as to please no one but a folklorist. According to one story, workmen digging gravel smashed what they had thought was a coconut and took the pieces to the tenant of a nearby manor. His daughter—later the raconteur of this self-serving tale—said he instructed the men to give them to Mr. Dawson. Dawson's own version was that he had asked the laborers to keep a sharp eye for any fossils and that they had later presented him with a small piece of a human parietal bone. A third version combines elements of the other two: A local antiquarian named W. J. Lewis Abbott maintained the workmen had smashed the "coconut" and thrown the pieces on the gravel heap where Dawson, "after a great deal of searching," had "recovered the first fragment." He added that Dawson did not know what he had found and so brought it to him for identification.[6]

Abbott's statements have helped place him on the roster of potential hoaxers. Those on it include a young Jesuit priest named Teilhard de Chardin (who joined Dawson in digging at the pit from 1909 to 1913); Sir Grafton Elliott Smith and Sir Arthur Keith (anatomists who promoted the authenticity of Piltown man); William J. Sollas (a paleontologist who also argued for Piltdown's authenticity); William Ruskin Butterfield (curator of a Sussex museum); Samuel A. Woodhead (a chemist and friend of Dawson); John T. Hewitt (a chemistry professor); and Martin A. C. Hinton (a volunteer worker at the British Museum); as well as others.[7]

Arthur Smith Woodward—distinguished geologist at the British Museum, to whom Dawson took his finds—has never been seriously considered a suspect, and rightly so for several reasons: his personal integrity, his lack of involvement with the Piltdown finds until years after the first fragment was recovered, and the fact that after Dawson's death Woodward dug extensively at Piltdown in a futile search for more traces of *Eoanthropus dawsoni.*[8]

There are also few grounds for suspecting any of the other men—notwithstanding the proliferating accusations. Teilhard de Chardin did not even meet Dawson until a year after the first bone fragment surfaced, and he was in France during the last three years of discoveries.[9] Some suspects have been supposed to have perpetrated the hoax to revenge themselves upon putative enemies: Butterfield against Dawson, or Sollas against Woodward. But if any trap was set, no one apparently attempted to spring it, and the "finds" were not proved fakes until 1953, long after the deaths of the presumed targets.

Besides, as Weiner demonstrates, if Dawson were the unwitting victim of an unknown hoaxer, the deceiver must have been "a figure of omnipotence not to be despised by Mephistopheles himself." That is because he would have to have had a seven-year "acquaintance with Dawson's movements and inquiries" that would be nothing less than "uncanny."[10]

Some writers have suggested that rather than representing a malicious hoax, the Piltdown affair began as a prank that simply got out of hand. Imagined pranksters include Teilhard, Smith, or a duo: Hewitt and Woodhead. However, the rational inquirer would seem compelled to agree with Charles Blinderman that "a seven-year joke seems a bit tedious."[11]

Just how absurd have become the attempts to "discover" the Piltdown perpetrator is illustrated by a 1982 article that accuses Sir Arthur Conan Doyle of the hoax. Cavalierly setting Dawson aside, the two authors of the doubly silly piece focus on the creator of Sherlock Holmes: Conan Doyle lived only a few miles from the Piltdown site! He even "appears to have visited it openly"! Moreover, he was "fascinated with the field of phrenology" and had a special knowledge of skulls! And there is more!—more such nonsense. The authors seem to have started with a suspect and then worked their way backward to the evidence.[12]

That is the approach of many would-be sleuths who turn out to be popular writers, editors, professors of biology and English—almost anything, it seems, but *investigators*—working on their first such case. One actually said of Dawson, "He is too obvious a culprit,"[13] a statement that sounds as if it was scripted for an episode of a TV mystery. *Real* detectives, of course, *look* for obvious culprits.

Such a figure is Charles Dawson, an English solicitor turned antiquarian and amateur geologist, whose numerous varied and unique finds made before his death in 1916 had earned him the appellation, the Wizard of Sussex.[14] As the announced discoverer of the cranial fragments and jawbone that constituted *Eoanthropus dawsoni,* Dawson came under suspicion after the hoax was uncovered in 1953, and considerable circumstantial evidence seemed to corroborate the suspicion.

Why, then, have some would-be investigators turned to other suspects? They argue that ultimately Dawson does not fit the profile they devise for the hoaxer. Especially do these theorists postulate someone with more scientific knowledge, notably in the realms of anthropology and chemistry, than they believe Dawson possessed. Also questioned are Dawson's ability to have obtained the particular bone specimens, as well as his willingness to have perpetrated such a hoax.[15]

However, the hoaxer's presumed high level of knowledge may be overstated. It is true that to produce a fossil ape-man's jaw from a modern orangutan's mandible required some alterations: breaking off the chin region and the bony knob (condyle) where the jaw articulates with the skull, and filing down the molars and canine teeth. Then, some cranial fragments had to be procured, the bones required staining to simulate age, and finally some prehistoric implements needed to be fashioned.[16]

Does this require consummate skill? As Stephen Jay Gould states:

Supporters of Dawson have maintained that a more professional scientist must have been involved, at least as a coconspirator, because the finds were so cleverly faked. I have always regarded this as a poor argument, advanced by scientists largely to assuage their embarrassment that such an indifferently designed hoax was not detected sooner. The staining, to be sure, had been done consummately. But the "tool" had been poorly carved and the teeth rather crudely filed— scratch marks were noted as soon as scientists looked with the right hypothesis in mind. Le Gros Clark wrote: "The evidences of artificial abrasion immediately spring to the eye. Indeed so obvious did they seem it may well be asked—how was it that they had escaped notice before?" The forger's main skill consisted in knowing what to leave out—discarding the chin and articulation.[17]

And Dawson was a knowledgeable amateur who, at the age of twenty-one, had become a Fellow of the Geological Society.[18] Besides, Dawson was able to benefit from the speculations of scientists prior to each new piece being found. For example, when the scientists wished that Piltdown man's canine tooth could be found having certain specific characteristics, Dawson's dig soon yielded one.

As to the staining—with potassium bichromate and iron sulfate solutions—the son of Dawson's friend, Samuel A. Woodhead, who was public analyst for East Sussex, stated: "Mr. Dawson asked my father how one would treat bones to make them appear older than they were and my father told him how it could be done. I would point out that my mother was present at this meeting."[19] Another Dawson friend and fellow amateur, Lewis Abbott, said he had assisted Dawson in staining the bones, which was done with the mistaken notion that the chemical would harden them. That rationale may have come from Dawson who did possess potassium bichromate.[20]

In 1915, Dawson allegedly found a second set of bones (known as Piltdown man II) having the fake iron and chromium staining, and at his death he had in his possession fragments of yet another skull, known as the Barcomb Mills skull, which at least one scientist thought was Piltdown III. It lacked a mandible, but was stained—artificially, with iron sulfate—to resemble Piltdown man.[21]

But could Dawson have obtained the necessary bones? He could. As Dawson defender Peter Costello concedes:

Even the orang jawbone would have presented little problem.

Borneo, the only source of such a bone, was a much visited place. The Hastings magnate, Lord Brassey, was there in his famous yacht Sunbeam—his collection can be seen today at the Hastings museum with which Dawson was connected. Brassey was a director of the British North Borneo Co.; another director lived in Eastbourne. In Brighton Museum today Bornean material from several private Sussex collections is on display. So in Sussex a medieval orang jawbone might easily have been found.[22]

Weiner likewise stated: "We can at once dispose of the notion that any difficulty would have been experienced in procuring an ape's mandible, or in all probability several, for the forger may have used up a number before he was satisfied. Then, as now, they could be bought from, or through, a local taxidermist, or, if not, then easily enough from one of the famous London firms."[23]

The presumption that Dawson would have been unlikely to risk exposure comes from Millar, who says: "The strain on the nerves would be too great. The threat of exposure would be perpetual."[24] But a similar argument might be made against anyone else, and *someone* faked the skull. Forgers, we know, tend to be endowed with "an exceptional amount of that type of courage which is best described as 'nerve.' "[25]

Not only *could* Dawson have perpetrated the Piltdown hoax, but he is also the likely suspect by almost any standard. And in this case there are several standards available. First, as shown in figure 13, he was the only person who was present at every find.[26] He either "discovered" the piece or was digging beside the one who did. For example, when Dawson's assistant, Teilhard, discovered the canine, Dawson was at his elbow. And when continental and American scientists doubted that the skull and mandible belonged to a single hominid, Dawson (so he claimed) dug at a new site and discovered the second set of bones. He failed to identify the site—if it actually existed—precisely thereby raising further suspicion about his guilt.[27]

Second, the discoveries of Piltdown relics, which had appeared at intervals since 1908, ceased immediately when Dawson fell ill in 1915 (only to die the following year). (See fig. 14.) Although Woodward's subsequent digs at the original site, conducted with the assistance of Grafton Elliot Smith and others, would have provided excellent opportunities for the persistent hoaxer to have struck again, nothing else was found at Piltdown. This suggests that either Dawson was the perpetrator, or that the hoaxer wished to victimize no one but Dawson. If the latter were the case, however, each suspect had many years before his own death (again see fig. 14) to have wreaked the ultimate revenge on a man unable to defend himself. He could have easily played up the hoax, either to ridicule Dawson as gullible victim or to make him out the perpetrator. Yet both hoax and hoaxer were silenced by Dawson's death.

The hoaxer may have had more than one motive. Perhaps, like many others of his ilk, he wished to fool the experts, making himself feel superior to them. (The Vermeer forger, Hans van Meegeren, angry at being ignored as an artist, wanted revenge on "the imperious rulers of the art world.")[28] In any event, Dawson had more to gain from the Piltdown hoax than anyone else. A discovery like *Eoanthropus dawsoni* would make him famous and probably would have earned him a knighthood but for his untimely death.[29] Such a possibility might blind a man to the risks involved.

Finally, there are Dawson's other finds—which range from the genuine, through the dubious, to the outright fake. Dawson wasn't called the Wizard of Sussex for nothing. He had to his credit three pre-Piltdown discoveries: a prehistoric reptile, mammal, and plant (each with *dawsoni* in its scientific name), but some who knew him thought him "proud," and his local reputation contrasted with the esteem accorded him by the scientists at the British Museum. According to Weiner,

It is common knowledge that Dawson did not command high esteem in the archaeological circle of Lewes [in Sussex]. Some local archae-ologists, on the basis of their personal feelings about Dawson as well as on their long-held, rather low opinion of his archaeological reliability, came to invest the Piltdown discovery with extreme skepticism from the start.[30]

In fact, by the time the canine tooth was discovered in 1913, some who knew him suspected that "Dawson was salting the mine."[31]

Peter Costello, who earlier wrote a book promoting belief in "lake monsters," defends Dawson against a charge of real-estate chicanery. Weiner accused Dawson of pretending to be purchasing Castle Lodge at Lewes for the Sussex Archaeological Society while actually acquiring it for himself. Details of the matter are disputed, but it is a fact that Dawson tendered his bid on the society's stationery.[32]

Costello also absolves Dawson of plagiarizing his 1909 book, *The History of Hastings Castle,* but Blinderman merely concludes that the accusation "stands as not proven." It is true that Dawson, in a preface, acknowledged making "free use" of an earlier, unpublished manuscript. However, as a contemporary reviewer wrote, "In many cases where matter is taken, mistakes and all, from earlier writings, no acknowledgment of the source is made."[33]

Moreover, as Alexander Kohn states in his *False Prophets:*

It seems that this was not the only case of literary piracy in which Dawson was involved. Dawson was an ardent collector of palaeontological material and of iron objects, which he exhibited in 1903 and 1908. In 1903 Dawson published an article about iron in *Sussex Archeological Collections* (5:46) in which 27 out of 61 pages were copied word for word from an earlier writer, Topley, to whom no acknowledgment was included.[34]

Nevertheless, Costello asserts that an examination of Dawson's "numerous investigations and publications reveals the interesting fact that with one possible exception all are honest and above board."[35] Costello's "possible exception" is a number of inscribed bricks that Dawson claimed to have personally excavated in 1902 at the Roman fort at Pevensey, Sussex. Stamped "HON AVG ANDRIA," the bricks thus appear to give the name of the Emperor Honorius, i.e., Honorius Augustus (r. A.D. 395–423)—and so provide evidence that the walls of the fort were refurbished during his reign. "Andria" was thought to uphold the view that the site's Roman name was Anderida.[36]

Unfortunately, the bricks do not match those "preserved in the walls of Pevensey," and the inscriptions are doubtful on stylistic grounds.[37] Worse, one of the bricks now in the British Museum was examined by thermoluminescence (a technique used to determine the age of fired clay and thus particularly important in dating pottery)[38] that demonstrated that the brick was not fired before about 1900.[39] Another of the Dawson bricks now in the Lewes Museum was also tested and revealed to be modern.[40]

The results are unfortunate for Dawson's reputation—unless one is willing to postulate that someone planted the fake bricks as well as the Piltdown bones, thus making it at least two people who tricked Dawson, or one who did it over a period totaling thirteen years.

Dawson also acquired other items for which he made grand claims, items that are now regarded as bogus: a "Roman" statuette that was supposed to be the earliest known example of the use of cast iron (but is probably a nineteenth-century curio),[41] a Norman "prick spur" (which, as the British Museum's Mark Jones says, "is no such thing"),[42] a prehistoric stag-horn "hammer" (of dubious attribution);[43] a "transitional horseshoe" (discounted, with other Dawson items, as having documentation that was "disquietingly faulty or vague");[44] an antique clock ("with a dial featuring a forged 17th c[entury] picture illustrating iron making");[45] and so on.

At one time or another, Dawson claimed to have seen a hybrid carp-goldfish; a horned horse; the skeleton of a new race of man that had a thirteenth vertebra; even a "sea-serpent" that he spied in the English Channel on Good Friday, 1906, and described with considerable detail.

Over and over, Dawson sought recognition through his fantastic "discoveries." In March 1909, in a letter to Woodward, he wrote that he was "waiting for the big discovery which never seems to come."[46] And then came Dawson's Dawn Man. . . .

Notes

1. Charles Blinderman, *The Piltdown Inquest* (Buffalo, N.Y.: Prometheus Books, 1986), 4.

2. William Broad and Nicholas Wade, *Betrayers of the Truth* (New York: Simon & Schuster, 1982), 120.

3. Ibid.; Ronald Millar, *The Piltdown Men* (London: Victor Gollanez, 1972), 30, 68–75, 81.

4. J. S. Weiner, *The Piltdown Forgery* (London: Oxford University Press, 1955), 204.

5. Ibid., 188.

6. Blinderman, *Piltdown Inquest,* 5–6; Weiner, *Piltdown Forgery,* 128–29.

7. Blinderman, *Piltdown Inquest,* 87. For Keith as a suspect, see John Noble Wilford, "Mastermind of Piltdown Hoax Unmasked?" *New York Times,* June 5, 1990.

8. Millar, *Piltdown Men,* 146.

9. Blinderman, *Piltdown Inquest,* 13; Weiner, *Piltdown Forgery,* 92.

10. Weiner, *Piltdown Forgery,* 200–202.

11. Blinderman, *Piltdown Inquest,* 87, 101.

12. John Hathaway Winslow and Alfred Meyer, "The Perpetrator at Piltdown," *Science* 83, no. 4 (September 1983): 33–43.

13. Millar, *Piltdown Men,* 226.

14. Weiner, *Piltdown Forgery,* 178.

15. Millar, *Piltdown Men,* 226–31; Blinderman, *Piltdown Inquest,* 13; Broad and Wade, *Betrayers of the Truth,* 121; Peter Costello, "The Piltdown Hoax Reconsidered," *Antiquity* 59 (1985): 172.

16. Weiner, *Piltdown Forgery,* 28–31, 54–69.

17. Stephen Jay Gould, "Piltdown Revisited," *Natural History* 88 (March 1979): 89.

18. Weiner, *Piltdown Forgery,* 85.

19. Lionel Woodhead, letter to Glyn Daniel, quoted in Costello, "Piltdown Hoax Reconsidered," 171.

20. Weiner, *Piltdown Forgery,* 148–50; Blinderman, *Piltdown Inquest,* 6–7, 202–204.

21. Robert Broom, "Summary of a Note on the Piltdown Skulls," *Advancement of Science* 24 (1950): 344; cited by Weiner, *Piltdown Forgery,* 151.

22. Costello, "Piltdown Hoax Reconsidered," 172.

23. Weiner, *Piltdown Forgery,* 108.

24. Millar, *Piltdown Men,* 227.

25. Charles E. O'Hara, *Fundamentals of Criminal Investigation,* 3rd ed. (Springfield, Ill.: Charles C. Thomas, 1973), 453.

26. Blinderman, *Piltdown Inquest,* 107. The information for the table is taken from Millar, *Piltdown Men,* 121–46; Weiner, *Piltdown Forgery,* 1–15; and Blinderman, *Piltdown Inquest,* 4–6, 13–15, 21–29, 49–50.

27. Weiner, *Piltdown Forgery,* 8–10, 77, 139; Blinderman, *Piltdown Inquest,* 50, 104.

28. Carlson Wade, *Great Hoaxes & Famous Imposters* (Middle Village, N.Y.: Jonathan David, 1976), 225.

29. Millar, *Piltdown Men,* 9.

30. Weiner, *Piltdown Forgery,* 169.

31. Captain Guy St. Barbe, quoted in Weiner, *Piltdown Forgery,* 166.

32. Costello, "Piltdown Hoax Reconsidered," 168–69; Blinderman, *Piltdown Inquest,* 109–110. Cf. Weiner, *Piltdown Forgery,* 173–75. Costello's earlier book was *In Search of Lake Monsters* (London: Garnstone Press, 1974).

33. Costello, "Piltdown Hoax Reconsidered," 168; Blinderman, *Piltdown Inquest,* 110–11; Weiner, *Piltdown Forgery,* 176 (quoting a reviewer for the *Sussex Archaeological Collections*).

34. Alexander Kohn, *False Prophets* (Cambridge, Mass.: Basil Blackwell, 1986), 150.

35. Costello, "Piltdown Hoax Reconsidered," 168.

36. Mark Jones, ed., *Fake? The Art of Deception* (London: British Museum Publications, 1990), 96; D. P. S. Peacock, "Forged Brick-stamps from Pevensey," *Antiquity* 47 (June 1973): 138.

37. Peacock, "Forged Brick-stamps," 139.

38. John FitzMaurice Mills, *Treasure Keepers* (New York: Doubleday, 1973), 39–45.

39. Peacock, "Forged Brick-stamps," 139.

40. Ibid.

41. Jones, *Fake?* 94–95; Weiner, *Piltdown Forgery,* 182.

42. Jones, *Fake?* 95; Weiner, *Piltdown Forgery,* 186.

43. Jones, *Fake?* 94, 96.

44. Weiner, *Piltdown Forgery,* 183.

45. David C. Devenish (former curator of Hastings Museum of Local History), letter to Joe Nickell, July 17, 1990.

46. Weiner, *Piltdown Forgery,* 178–82; Jones, *Fake?* 94; Blinderman, *Piltdown Inquest,* 109.

Select Bibliograhy

Costello, Peter. "The Piltdown Hoax Reconsidered." *Antiquity* 59 (1985): 167–73. Defense of Dawson as one wrongfully suspected of faking the Piltdown skull.

Jones, Mark, ed. *Fake? The Art of Deception.* London: British Museum Publications, 1990. Survey of fakes, including other bogus artifacts by Charles Dawson.

Weiner, J. S. *The Piltdown Forgery.* London: Oxford University Press, 1955. The original and still the standard text on the Piltdown mystery.

Winslow, John Hathaway, and Oscar Meyer. "The Perpetrator at Piltdown." *Science* 83, no. 4 (September 1983): 33–43. Absurd attempt to accuse Sir Arthur Conan Doyle of perpetrating the Piltdown hoax.

Acknowledgments

Among the many who helped with our investigation, we are especially grateful to David C. Devenish (former curator of Hastings Museum of Local History) for his suggestions, and to Catherine Johns (Curator, Department of Prehistoric and Romano-British Antiquities, The British Museum) for valuable research assistance.

9

Miraculous Blood
(Investigated with John F. Fischer)

Religious zealots call it a "miracle," yet a writer for *New Scientist* notes it is a "flawed miracle," and *The Oxford Dictionary of Saints* terms it an "alleged" one.[1] A spokesman for the Catholic Church states, "It may not be a miracle, but whatever it is, it somehow functions outside the realm of ordinary laws."[2] Skeptics have asserted it is nothing more than a magic trick, with one criticizing "this paltering with religion."[3] To still other observers, it is simply a mystery, or "just another of those unsolved enigmas associated with holy places and objects."[4]

What is at issue is the nature of the phenomenon produced by a vial of "blood" reposing in a Naples cathedral. According to the testimony of eyewitnesses dating back to at least the fourteenth century, what is represented as the congealed blood of a martyred saint periodically liquefies, reddens, and froths—in apparent contravention of natural laws. (See fig. 15.)

But does such a transformation really occur and, if so, is it a mystery beyond the ken of science? Or does it result from some hitherto unexplained physical process, or even outright trickery? To answer these and other questions, we initiated an investigation of the "miracle" that spanned several years and consisted of three major phases: (1) researching the provenance of the vials, including their legendary source; (2) studying the observed phenomena; and (3) conducting relevant laboratory experiments. This is the first published report on our findings.

The Legend

Little is known about San Gennaro—Saint Januarius, the martyr whose alleged blood undergoes the remarkable metamorphosis. According to popular tradition, he was born at Naples near the close of the third century and was bishop of Benevento when the Roman emperor Diocletian began persecuting Christians. In A.D. 305, upon visiting a friend and his companions who had been imprisoned for their faith, Januarius was also imprisoned. After they were thrown to the lions (or bears, as another version states) who refused to harm them (or when, according to another legend, they were cast into a fiery furnace yet remained uninjured), they were beheaded at Pozzuoli.

In fact, however, although Januarius is the patron saint of Naples, the Chruch has never been able to document his existence as an actual historical personage. No contemporary reference to him has been located; neither does his name appear in any of the early Roman martyrologies. As a consequence, during the Roman Catholic Cultural Revolution of the 1960s, the importance of Januarius was greatly diminished, along with such legendary figures as Saint Christopher, the popular protector of travelers, and Saint George, the dragon slayer.[5]

Januarius's reputed bones were disinterred in the fifth century and lodged in Naples, then shifted to various locales in Italy over the next several centuries. The relics—or what were alleged to be them—were returned to Naples in the later thirteenth century when Charles II of

Anjou, King of Naples, built a cathedral there to enshrine the saint's skull.

Such veneration of martyrs' relics was widespread and received theological endorsement on the grounds that God worked miracles through them. So prevalent had the practice become even by the time of Saint Augustine (ca. 400) that he decried "hypocrites in the garb of monks" for "hawking about of the limbs of martyrs," adding skeptically, "if indeed of martyrs."[6] Indeed, in the Middle Ages,

> The living bodies of likely future saints were covetously watched by relic mongers; when Thomas Aquinas fell ill and died at a French monastery [in 1274], his body was decapitated and his flesh boiled away by monks greedy for his bones. It is said that Saint Romuald of Ravenna heard during a visit to France that he was in mortal peril because of the value of his bones—he fled homeward, pretending to be mad.[7]

In 1337, ceremonies held in honor of the "head of the most holy Januarius"—by then encased in a silver reliquary—were formalized in a liturgical constitution written by the Neapolitan archbishop, Giovanni Orsini. Although the document carefully details the proscribed ritual, there is no mention of the vials of blood, not even an allusion to them nor any hint of the alleged miracle.

Indeed, there is absolutely no historical record for the saint's blood prior to 1389, in which year, on August 17, an unknown traveler reported his astonishment at witnessing the liquefaction. The suspicions that naturally follow from this lack of provenance increase when another fact is considered: There are additional saints' bloods that liquefy, some twenty in all, and virtually every one of them is found in the Naples area. For example, reports Guerdon:

> We note in the Neapolitan hagiography a great number of holy personages who, having been bled after their death, gave forth blood that was fresh and liquid. This blood, enclosed in a phial or collected

on a cloth, becomes a relic and causes numerous marvels and miracles.
So it is with St. Andrew Avellino (died in 1608), with Bd. Bonaventure
of Potenza (died in 1711), with St. Francis de Geronimo (died in 1716),
with the venerable Giambattista of Borgogna (died at the age of twenty-
six in 1726), with Father Cesare Sportelli (died in 1750), with Father
Latessa (died in 1755), with St. Gerard Majella (died in 1755), etc.[8]

Such proliferation—which a skeptical Father Herbert Thurston
termed "a rather useless manifestation of the divine omnipotence"[9]—
seems less suggestive of the miraculous than indicative of some regional
secret. In fact, according to James Hansen:

[H]istory records that Raimondo of San Severo, a Neapolitan alchem-
ist and doubter of the 17th century, managed to duplicate the miracle
and habitually performed it for house guests by way of a party trick.
This may have been a contributing cause of his eventual excommuni-
cation.[10]

It is in this skeptical light that one must view the improbable—
if pious—little legend about the acquisition of the saint's blood. Tradition
holds that Januarius's nurse, Eusebia, was present at his beheading and
immediately preserved some of his blood in two vials. These were
subsequently taken with his remains to the Neapolitan catacombs. In-
serted in the urn containing his bones, the blood supposedly liquefied
immediately. However, this legend has an even shorter history than the
vials, failing to appear until the second half of the sixteenth century.

Another legend concerns the stone upon which the execution was
allegedly carried out (or, alternately, since it features an oblong cavity,
the basin in which Eusebia washed her bloodstained hands). Housed
in the monastery church at Pozzuoli, the block of marble stands in
a niche where lighting and viewing conditions are not the best. Nevertheless, at least "under electric light" the stone's cavity "seems" to be
"reddish brown, with unevenly distributed spots." The cavity supposedly reddens when Januarius's blood liquefies in Naples (although sub-

jectivity, the power of suggestion, and focused lighting may be responsible), and "people say" it sometimes exudes blood, as it reportedly did
in 1860 and again in 1894.[11]

One of the bits of cotton supposedly used to sponge off the blood
on the latter occasion was tested and reported to be human blood (with
no miraculous properties being indicated). However, Guerdon concedes
the possibility of fraud, and one is reminded of the many cases of
"bleeding" icons that have turned out to be hoaxes. (There was Rose
Tamisier, for example, a French stigmatic who claimed to receive visits
from the Virgin Mary and who caused a picture of Christ to emit "real
blood." She was tried in 1851 and convicted of imposture.[12] A more
recent example occurred in Quebec in 1985 when a small statue of the
Virgin wept tears and then blood. The "miracle" drew some 12,000 people
in less than a week, but it was soon exposed as a hoax: a mixture of
fat and blood flowed when the room the statue was in became heated.)[13]

Adding to the suspicion that the Pozzuoli phenomenon is a hoax
are the facts that the stone actually comes from a sixth-century marble
altar and that the red traces are residues of old paint![14] Moreover, the
story of the Pozzuoli stone exhibits *motifs* (narrative elements) that are
common to legends and well known to folklore study: revenant [i.e.,
ghost] as "blood" and "ineradicable bloodstain after bloody tragedy."
Moreover, as Guerdon states: "It is regrettable that no analysis of the
phenomenon has yet been made with sufficient scientific control"; in
any case, authorities indicate that "the exudations would tend to be
less evident nowadays."[15]

Reasonably considered, the evidence from the relics' provenance—
or rather the glaring lack thereof—together with the proliferation of
similar miracles in the Neapolitan region, casts grave doubt on either
the vials of "blood" or the Pozzuoli stone having any historic link with
San Gennaro. Nevertheless, something remarkable seems to be occurring with the vials; despite the dubious circumstances surrounding them,
is the phenomenon a paranormal one after all?

The Januarian Phenomenon

As the late D. Scott Rogo stated in his *Miracles: A Parascientific Inquiry into Wondrous Phenomena* (1982), the miracle associated with St. Januarius "is a scientific puzzle as well as a religious one," and more reports have been written concerning it than any other miracle of the Catholic Church.[16] Although sustained scientific scrutiny of the phenomenon has never been permitted,[17] some analyses of questionable merit have been conducted. These, together with observations made over the centuries plus videotapes of the phenomenon that we were able to study, serve as a basis for attempting to assess the alleged miracle.

In earlier times the reliquary containing the supposed blood was stored in a locked niche in an old section of the Naples Cathedral, but today it is kept in a special vault in an interior chapel. It contains two vials of unequal size: the larger, pear-shaped ampule, flattened front and back, has an estimated sixty-cubic-centimeter capacity and is about half full; the adjacent cylindrical vial has a capacity of about twenty-five cubic centimeters but is empty, except for a few spots of the substance remaining on the glass. (This vial was supposedly opened in the eighteenth century and its contents given to wealthy Neapolitan families, as well as Philip V of Spain; however, these gifts cannot be substantiated.)

The vials are embedded in a dark putty that attached them to an internal silver crown dating from the fourteenth century. This in turn is contained in a cylindrical silver case of the seventeenth century. Measuring about twelve centimeters (about 4¾ inches) in diameter, the case is enclosed by two circular pieces of clear glass about eight centimeters apart, permitting the vials to be viewed from either side. The case also has a handle by which it can be held in the hand or fitted into an ornate monstrance that supports it.

The Januarian ritual takes place several times annually, notably on the Saturday preceding the first Sunday in May (to commemorate the relics' entry into Naples) and the eight days following it, and during the octave beginning on September 19 (the saint's feast day, the anniversary of his legendary death)—a total of seventeen days. The ritual was formerly performed also on December 16 (in commemoration of the great eruption of Mount Vesuvius in 1631, at which time the blood reportedly remained liquid for thirty days); however, the liquefaction occurred "much more rarely" on this date, and it was discontinued in 1971. The "miracle" has also been invoked "at the time of the visits of distinguished persons, or when the relics are exhibited to fend off calamities."[18]

During the ritual, a priest exposes the blood relics before the other reliquary, which is said to contain the martyr's skull but seems only to contain small bone fragments. The vials are held aloft while the congregation prays and beseeches, "Saint Januarius, delight us!" or "Give us our miracle!" If that is not forthcoming, those in attendance are not adverse to rudely cajoling the saint. Usually after a period of about half an hour to an hour, the phenomenon suddenly occurs, greeted by cheers and applause. A dignitary approaches with a flashlight so the faithful can better see the liquefaction.[19]

Descriptions of the liquefaction vary, and it is not always easy to separate what may be permutations in the phenomenon's occurrence from differences attributable to individual perceptions. (Whether inconsistency is compatible with the miraculous is a question we leave to theologians.) One modern eyewitness report was given by a Naples physician, Dr. Giorgio Giorgi, in a 1970 Italian parapsychology journal. He described how the case was held up and slowly rotated; then, he stated:

> After about four minutes, certainly no longer, I was disconcerted to see just in front of my nose, at a distance of little over three feet, that the clot of blood had suddenly changed from the solid state into that of a liquid. The transformation from solid into liquid happened suddenly and unexpectedly. The liquid itself had become much brighter, more shining; so many gaseous bubbles appeared inside the liquid (shall we call it blood?) that is seemed to be in a state of ebullition.[20]

What Giorgi qualifies as *seemingly* ebullient, however, others characterize by saying the blood "melts, bubbles up, and flows down the sides of the vials" or even that it "bubbles and boils."[21] Still others, however, using less emotionally charged wording, merely say that the substance is seen to "froth."[22] Additional features of the Januarian phenomenon are reported. In answer to skeptics who have suggested the liquefaction results from increased temperature (attributed to nearby candles and electric lights, or to body heat from those in the chapel, even to warmth from the priest's hands), proponents of paranormal hypotheses counter that the phenomenon acts independently of temperature and sometimes occurs more readily in September than in May.

Besides, blood would actually be accelerated in its coagulation if heat were applied, and tests supposedly show the substance is blood. In 1902 and again more recently, researchers were permitted to tilt the reliquary so as to pass a beam of light through the film that remained on the inner wall of the vial. They claimed their resulting spectroscopic analysis proved the presence of genuine blood.[23]

It is also maintained that, after its liquefaction, the substance exhibits variations in volume and weight. The normal level in the vial can either rise or fall; also sometimes the weight decreases when the volume *increases,* and vice versa. Such data, states Guerdon, "go outside all the physical laws," and "are avoided by the rationalist scholars."[24]

Finally, the substance does more than just liquefy. In addition to the reported color change from dark to bright, it may undergo other transformations. States Rogo:

> Its viscosity also goes through a sequence of variations, becoming abnormally pasty just before liquefying and then much more viscous than normal blood. Occasionally not all of the matter will liquefy, but a central "ball" or clot will remain solid and bob about in the middle of the blood. This central clot is one of the more peculiar aspects of the manifestation. Witnesses have testified that it will actually exude liquefied blood—and absorb the blood as it resolidifies—as though serving as a sort of "filter" for the miracle.[25]

When, on occasion the blood fails to liquefy, tradition holds that disaster is imminent. After one such failure, pressed to identify the threat, the archbishop of Naples named "neopaganism"; his flock interpreted this "as an oblique but unmistakable reference to the rise of Italian Communism."[26] If that seems strained, one finds even less logic in the fact (mentioned earlier) that during the terrible eruption of Vesuvius in 1631—when the blood would have been supposed to have remained congealed—the reputed barometer of tragedy gave an incredibly false response: while some 18,000 perished, the substance liquefied and remained so for thirty days.[27]

We looked critically at all these alleged aspects of the Januarian phenomenon, attempting to avoid the approaches of others that seemed to us to fall largely into two categories: those attempting either to promote religious belief or to foster mystery for whatever reasons, and those who would dismiss the matter out of hand or provide only a superficial explanation for the reported occurrences. Ours would be an attempt to solve the enigma.

Science of Miracles

As we have seen, responses to the liquefaction are at great variance; so are notions about the cause. For example, the Catholic writer Leon Cavène, writing in 1909 about earlier observations, found it "most remarkable" that "modern science" had been enlisted to prove "the supernatural character of the Miracle of St. Januarius." Cavène held that the various alleged features of the phenomenon proved the existence of God, the existence of the human soul and its survival at death, the legitimacy of "the cult of saints," and, ultimately, the "divine mission" of the Catholic Church.[28] (The Church itself, however, makes no such claims regarding the phenomenon. States Spraggett, "No Catholic is obliged to believe in the miracle of the blood of St. Januarius, and many outspokenly don't.")[29]

On the other hand, Hans Bender, a German parapsychologist, compared the liquefaction to alleged paranormal manifestations that are popularly termed "hauntings." Bender suggested that the emotional force accompanying Saint Januarius's beheading *somehow* imbued the blood with a psychic energy that, in turn, *somehow* produced the liquefaction.[30] Rogo, however, noted that "haunted houses seem to 'act up' cyclically—ghosts will be seen and mysterious noises will be heard for a while, but then the houses will go into a period of quiescence that may last several months before the ruckus begins again." Rogo urged consideration of another factor, suggesting that "The intense religious fervor of the crowds gathered to witness the miracle in Naples might catalyze a preexisting psychic field dormant in the blood, thus causing the clot to liquefy."[31]

We find all such speculations premature, to say the least. The tone of so-called "miraculists"[32] like Cavène gives one the impression that their eyes glaze over whenever they contemplate the mix of magic and the macabre that they attribute to the blood relics. And parapsychologists like Bender are attempting to "explain" the unknown by the unproved. Our own view is that one should not invoke a supernatural or paranormal explanation until all natural or human agencies have been decisively ruled out. As we shall see, notwithstanding the assertions of some who have rushed to judgment on the matter, that has by no means occurred.

Take, for example, the assertions that the substance is genuine blood, assertions predicated solely on the spectroscopic analyses. The 1902 tests were conducted by Gennaro Sperindeo, a priest and physicist, and Raffaele Januario, a professor of chemistry at the University of Naples—neither, so far as we know, an expert either in the identification of blood substances or in spectroscopy. (Indeed, the statement that the pair "procured a good spectroscope"[33] suggests such work may have been new to them.) The more recent tests were done by "a team of Italian medical researchers," but limitations on the analyses cast grave doubts on their work: As pointed out by various scientists, not only did their light beam have to pass through the two glass plates of the reliquary and the two curved layers of the vial, but antiquated equipment was used instead of a modern electronic spectrophotometer. Moreover, even if the findings of the Neapolitan researchers were accepted at face value, the possibility of other substances being present would have to be acknowledged, and the researchers themselves admit that certain dyes could even be mistaken for hemoglobin.[34]

Further doubt is cast on the results of the spectral analyses, at least from a scientific viewpoint, by the fact that the "blood" does not otherwise seem to be blood. Based on our own observations of two professional quality color videotapes of the phenomenon,[35] the liquid was rather thick, altogether more viscous than genuine blood. More significantly, real blood would, of course, remain dark and coagulated. To call that which is inconsistent with blood "miraculous blood" is to engage in intellectual dishonesty—until, perhaps (as was observed during the Turin "shroud" controversy), a science of miracles is developed. (When shroud proponents postulated radiation as the mechanism that formed the image of Christ on his alleged burial cloth, skeptical scientists countered that no known radiation had the requisite properties; but authenticity advocates invoked a miracle and invented a resurrection "radiance.")[36]

In addition to the analyses of the "blood," there are also serious problems with the weighings of the vial that are supposed to prove the substance therein changes weight. Those measurements—made by Sperindeo in 1902 and by a Father Silva in 1904—were at best "rather crude."[37] While there were reported variations of almost twenty-seven grams in 1902 and over ten grams in 1904, the measurements were made over a period of several days each while the temperature in the cathedral "oscillated" and the humidity went unrecorded. Moreover, since the vial could not be removed, the entire case had to be weighed, yielding a maximum figure (in 1902) of about 1,015 grams. Therefore, rather than the vial's contents varying considerably—as much, it is alleged, as 100 percent[38]—the fact is that the weight of the *reliquary* varied by about 2.7 percent in 1902 and only about one percent in 1904. In addition to the problem of loading an analytical balance with such a heavy weight—five times that recommended[39]—and of other potential problems (such as convective currents in the cathedral), fluctuations in weight are attributable to other factors, with added moisture, such as might be absorbed by the case's putty, being just one possibility. In any event a recent authority reports that "Tests performed during the last five years by using electric balances failed to confirm any weight variation."[40]

Further undermining claims made for the weight measurements are those concerning fluctuations in volume. Cavène attempted to equate the two, characterizing the overall difference in weight as "corresponding to the difference in the volume." He saw the one as corroborating the other and together pointing to a miracle.[41] However, as we have seen, other proponents have noted that, within each several days' weighing period, *the weight increased whereas the volume decreased,* while sometimes, on the contrary, *the weight decreased whereas the volume increased,*" observations made originally by Sperindeo and Silva. These changes are often cited as even greater proof of the miraculous or the paranormal, but—as Guerdon further observes—the variations in volume and weight "are not proportional" and therefore "apparently are independent of one another."[42] Considered scientifically, they beg the question of whether either set of contradictory claims is valid.

We did not observe the alleged changes in volume, but the observations of others can be explained without recourse to the supernatural. A clue comes from researcher Arnaldo Giaccio who in 1907 postulated that the apparent increase was merely "an illusion" caused by the "viscous, syrupy" liquid coating the upper portion of the vial and appearing as "an enormous augmentation of volume." He claimed to have reproduced the effect. Cavène, however, protested that the liquid is not sufficiently viscous for Giaccio's hypothesis and that, anyway, liquid clinging to the interior wall of the vial when the reliquary is moved about is not opaque.[43] Finally, we should note that, according to a recent authority, "volume variations seem to be no longer reported."[44]

Our own suggestion is based on the observation that the substance in the vial can apparently recongeal as quickly as it frequently seems to liquefy. Indeed, "the blood often solidifies during the procession, despite the jarring of the vial."[45] If the reliquary was being swirled about when the material began to congeal, it could—in a thickened and thus opaque film—coat the upper portion of the vial to any height; it could even give the appearance that the vial was full. According to Coulson, "there is no means of telling whether the mass is solid throughout, or whether empty space is enclosed within a solid crust thus accounting for the apparent variation in volume."[46]

This hypothesis is supported by the observation of a Professor Fergola who wrote: "Often, the blood expands a great deal, so much that one cannot see whether it is fluid, no matter how one turns the vial." Similarly, on another occasion an observer reported the substance so filled the vial "that it was impossible to know if it was solid or liquid." Partial liquefying and recongealing, repeated over several days' handling, could even cause the substance to appear to rise gradually in the vial, as has been reported on rare occasions.[47]

Then there are the assertions that the substance "boils." According to Larcher, the expression is "inexact." He states, "There is no actual boiling, simply a formation of foam." As he explains, the substance "only occasionally" yields "little bubbles that group themselves in foam on the surface of the substance after liquefaction."[48] Could this foaming not be merely a consequence of the liquid being agitated when, the liquefaction having just occurred, "the priest waves the vial triumphant-ly"?[49] Such an effect can easily be demonstrated by shaking a partially filled bottle of (say) olive oil. Or, since the substance sometimes re-solidifies during the subsequent procession when the reliquary is again subject to agitation, could not bubbles become entrapped in the con-gealed substance, only to be released upon the next liquefaction?

As to the substance changing color "from dark red to bright red,"[50] that appears to correlate exactly with the liquefaction. Therefore, we feel that it is simply due to the fact that when the substance is congealed no light passes through it and it is viewed only in reflected light. However, when it has liquified and a candle is held behind the case, light is transmitted through the vial. Thus the "blood" seems (as Dr. Giorgi was quoted earlier as saying) "Much brighter, more shining."

Finally, there is the liquefaction itself, the essential Januarian phenom-enon, which has been the subject of literally centuries of debate. Skeptics have long suspected that whatever the substance in the vials is, it is susceptible to melting whenever the reliquary is sufficiently warmed. Although this is denied by the miraculists—who point out that the phenomenon sometimes occurred in December but not in May when the temperature was warmer—it is also true that it took place more often in May and September, and that the December event was discontinued. In addition, as a skeptical Father Thurston pointed out concerning the other liquefying blood relics in the Naples area, the feast days of all of the saints involved fall in the warm season.[51]

Actually, the subject of temperature is much more complex than is implied by a discussion of the time of year involved. Of more obvious significance than the outdoor temperature is the indoor one. While it is true that the miraculists publish tables presumably demonstrating a lack of constant relationship between church temperature and the time it takes for liquefaction to occur, they completely ignore a multiplicity of additionally relevant factors. For example, what was the temperature of the reliquary in its niche (or in recent years, its vault), and how long had it been at that temperature before being brought to the proximity of electric lights, candles, people, and other thermally radiating sources?

Other factors to be considered are the humidity, the thermal conductivity of the surface the reliquary rests on in its vault, the heat of the hands holding the reliquary (a source of heat apparently not applied to the thermometer used by Neapolitan researchers), and many other factors. Suffice it to say that, despite the scientific appearance fostered by publishing multi-column tables, scientific rigor has scarcely made its acquaintance with the Januarian phenomenon.

What can be said, by way of approximation, is that the liquefaction seems to occur at about the room temperature of the chapel, about 19–27° centigrade (or about 66.2–80.6° Fahrenheit), and after the lapse of varying times depending on certain physical factors. Rationalist scholar Pierre Saintyves insisted the liquefaction never takes place when the temperature is below 17° centigrade.[52]

Saintyves theorized that the substance was blood, to which, to prevent decomposition, some preservative such as "essence of balsam or aromatic resin" had been added.[53] A mixture of blood and wax has also been suggested,[54] as have additional concoctions: blood and chalk; an aqueous suspension of chocolate powder, casein, and other ingredients; a mixture of tallow, ether, and carmine; and so on.[55]

Not surprisingly, there were problems: of homogeneity (the tallow mixture stratified into three layers); of effect (for example, one experimental vial had to be heated in a candle flame); of history (neither chocolate nor ether or carmine was available in the fourteenth century); and of the probable effects of age (resins, for example, might harden over time).

A more successful recipe was supplied by Pierre Larousse in his nineteenth-century *Universal Dictionary:* "sulfuric ether reddened with plant Alkanna Tinctoria and the obtained dye saturated with spermacetti." We only recently learned of Larousse's mixture, which was reconsituted by Henri Broch and reported as "reproducing *all* aspects of the miracle of Naples."[56]

We offer our own "generic" solution to the problem. As a "thought experiment" consider a vial half-filled with a nondrying oil (e.g., olive oil) that will remain liquid at even cool temperatures. To it is added a substance (e.g., melted beeswax) that forms a mixture that is normally congealed at room temperature. Only a small amount of this is added, sufficient that when the whole is cool, the mixture is solid, but when slightly warmed, the trace of congealing substance melts and—slowly or even quite suddenly—the mixture liquefies. A pigment must be added, say, dragonsblood, known from classical times and popular in the Middle Ages.[57]

This hypothesis would seem consistent with the Januarian features. For example, the central "ball" (or *globo* as the Italians speak of it) that sometimes remains undissolved or dissolves slowly (like a pat of butter melting in a skillet) is suggestive of a substance that liquefies by melting.

Actually, rather than employ such an oil-and-wax mixture, there are substances that already have the sharp temperature gradient necessary to reproduce the Januarian phenomenon—coconut oil, for example.

Along such lines, we have produced our own vials of "blood" (dubbed

"Saint Februarius") that perform with sufficient success to permit us to say this: However accurately we may have guessed the secret, we will wager we are much closer to the formula than anything proposed by the paranormalists.[58] As Coulson states: "A very important fact is that liquefaction has occurred during repair of the casket, a circumstance in which it seems highly unlikely that God would work a miracle."[59]

In 1991, before we could publish our research, a team of Italian scientists made international headlines with their own solution to the Januarian mystery. Writing in the journal *Nature,* Prof. Luigi Garlaschelli (Department of Organic Chemistry, University of Pavia) and two colleagues from Milan, Franco Ramaccini and Sergio Della Sala, proposed "that thixotropy may furnish an explanation." A thixotropic gel is one capable of liquefying when agitated and of resolidifying when allowed to stand. The Italian scientists created such a gel by mixing chalk and hydrated iron chloride with a small amount of salt water and reported a convincing replication of the Januarian phenomena.[60] (See figs. 16 and 17.)

In response, Bernard J. Leikind, a physicist who had been kind enough to review our work, commented that he found the Italians' idea "plausible, as is the one that you considered." While noting that the precise answer "cannot be decided until tests on the material are made," Leikind concluded: "The real point is that since there are at least two plausible naturalistic explanations for the liquefaction, both well within the range of normal behavior of materials, there is no reason to require divine intervention."[61]

Notes

1. Except as otherwise indicated, information in this chapter is taken from an English translation (provided by Scott Rogo) of David Guerdon, "Le Sang de Saint Janvier se liquefie et se cogule depuis des siecles," *Psi International Bimestrial* 5 (1978): 9–29. See also D. Scott Rogo, *Miracles: A Parascientific Inquiry into Wondrous Phenomena* (New York: Dial, 1982), 186–202; James

Hansen, "Can Science Allow Miracles?" *New Scientist* (April 8, 1982): 73–76; David Hugh Farmer, *The Oxford Dictionary of Saints* (Oxford: Clarendon, 1978), 208.

2. Kathrine Jason, "Bubbling Blood," *Omni* (July 1982): 92.

3. E. Cobham Brewer, *A Dictionary of Miracles* (Philadelphia: Lippincott, 1884), 184.

4. Colin Wilson, *Enigmas and Mysteries* (New York: Doubleday, 1976), 125.

5. Hansen, "Can Science Allow Miracles?" 74; John Coulson, ed., *The Saints: A Concise Biographical Dictionary* (New York: Hawthorn, 1958), 238.

6. "Relics," *Encyclopaedia Britannica* (1973).

7. Karl E. Meyer, "Were You There When They Photographed My Lord?" *Esquire* (August 1971): 73.

8. Guerdon, "Le Sang de Saint Janvier" (see n. 1).

9. Quoted in Guerdon, "Le Sang de Saint Janvier."

10. Hansen, "Can Science Allow Miracles?" 74.

11. Guerdon, "Le Sang de Saint Janvier."

12. Ibid.; Brewer, *Dictionary of Miracles,* 184–85.

13. Joe Nickell with John F. Fischer, *Secrets of the Supernatural* (Buffalo, N.Y.: Prometheus Books, 1988), 120.

14. Ennio Moscarella, *Il sangue di S. Gennaro vescovo e martire* (1989), cited by Prof. Luigi Garlaschelli, et al., letter to Joe Nickell, Nov. 5, 1991.

15. Stith Thompson, *Motif-Index of Folk Literature,* rev. ed., 6 vol. (Bloomington: Indiana Univ. Press, 1955), 2:446; Guerdon, "Le Sang de Saint Janvier."

16. Rogo, *Miracles.*

17. Hansen, "Can Science Allow Miracles?" 74.

18. Guerdon, "Le Sang de Saint Janvier" (see n. 1).

19. Coulson, *Saints,* 239; Allen Spraggett, " 'Miracle' of the Blood of St. Januarius," *Toronto Sun,* Aug. 16, 1972: 6; Rogo, *Miracles,* 186–202; G. B. Alfano and A. Amitrano, *Il Miracolo di San Gennaro* (Naples: Scarpati, 1950), 150.

20. Giorgio Giorgi, quoted in translation in Rogo, *Miracles,* 193.

21. John J. Delaney, *Dictionary of Saints* (Garden City, N.Y.: Doubleday, 1980), 310–11.

22. Spraggett, " 'Miracle' of the Blood of St. Januarius," 6; Coulson,

Saints, 239.

23. Guerdon, "Le Sang de Saint Janvier"; Leon Cavène, *Le celebre Miracle de Saint Janvier a Naples et a Pouzzoles* (Paris: Gabriel Beauchesne, 1909), 258ff; "Miracle: Blood Passes Scientific Test," *Our Sunday Visitor,* Jan. 7. 1990.

24. Guerdon, "Le Sang de Saint Janvier."

25. Rogo, *Miracles.*

26. "Starting Out on a Journey of No Return," *Time,* May 17, 1976, 25.

27. Arthur H. Norway, *Naples: Past and Present* (New York: Frederick A. Stokes, 1901), 2:12–14; "Vesuvius," *Encyclopaedia Britannica* (1960).

28. Cavène, *Le celebre Miracle de Saint Janvier,* 346.

29. Spraggett, " 'Miracle' of the Blood of St. Januarius," 6.

30. Cited in Guerdon, "Le Sang de Saint Janvier."

31. Rogo, *Miracles.*

32. The term *miraculistes* (in French) is given in Hubert Larcher, *Le Sang: Peut-Il Vaincre la Mort?* (N.p.: Librairie Gallimard, 1957), 281.

33. Cavène, *Le celebre Miracle de Saint Janvier,* 258.

34. "Miracle" (n. 23); Cavène, *Le celebre Miracle de Saint Janvier,* 258ff; Guerdon, "Le Sang de Saint Janvier." In addition to our own criticisms, there are those of Luigi Garlaschelli (Department of Organic Chemistry, University of Pavia) and Franco Ramaccini and Sergio Della Sala (his colleagues from Milan), given in their letter to Joe Nickell, Nov. 5, 1991.

35. These were aired on the television shows "You Asked for It," Dec. 27, 1982, and "Ripley's Believe It or Not," Oct. 24, 1982.

36. Joe Nickell, *Inquest on the Shroud of Turin,* 2nd updated ed. (Buffalo, N.Y.: Prometheus Books, 1988), 85–94.

37. Guerdon, "Le Sang de Saint Janvier."

38. Cavène, *Le celebre Miracle de Saint Janvier,* 333–38; Spraggett, " 'Miracle' of the Blood of St. Januarius," 6.

39. William Marshall MacNevin, *The Analytical Balance: Its Care and Use* (Sandusky, Oh.: Handbook Publi., 1951), 25.

40. Moscarella, *Il sangue di S. Gennaro,* 401 (see n. 14).

41. Cavène, *Le celebre Miracle de Saint Janvier,* 338.

42. Guerdon, "Le Sang de Saint Janvier" (see n. 1).

43. Cavène, *Le celebre Miracle de Saint Janvier,* 319.

44. Moscarella, *Il sangue di S. Gennaro,* 401 (see n. 14).

45. Guerdon, "Le Sang de Saint Janvier."

46. Coulson, *Saints,* 239.

47. Quoted in Larcher, *Le Sang,* 274; Cavène, *Le celebre Miracle de Saint Janvier,* 301ff.

48. Larcher, *Le Sang,* 277.

49. Spraggett, " 'Miracle' of the Blood of St. Januarius," 6.

50. Larcher, *Le Sang,* 278.

51. Guerdon, "Le Sang de Saint Janvier."

52. Quoted in Larcher, *Le Sang,* 289.

53. Ibid.

54. Farmer, *Oxford Dictionary of Saints,* 208.

55. Guerdon, "Le Sang de Saint Janvier."

56. Henri Broch, "New-Old Insight into the 'Bloody Miracle' of San Gennaro," *Skeptical Inquirer* 17 (Fall 1992): 91–93.

57. Daniel V. Thompson, *The Materials and Techniques of Medieval Painting* (New York: Dover, 1956), 124–26.

58. Since, as we have seen, many of the phenomena attributed to St. Januarius's "blood" are dubious, or may simply be due to such relatively minor factors as viscosity, a particular pigment (which may have altered in color over time), etc., for our vials we focused primarily on producing an approximately blood-colored substance that successfully reproduces the liquefying and congealing effect.

59. Coulson, *Saints,* 239.

60. Luigi Garlaschelli et al., letter to *Nature* 353 (Oct. 10, 1991): 507; "Scientists say 'Miracle' No Mystery," *Chicago Tribune,* Oct. 19, 1991; "Shakeup Over Sacred Blood," *Science News,* Oct. 12, 1991: 229.

61. Bernard J. Leikind, letter to Joe Nickell, Nov. 4, 1991.

Select Bibliography

Cavène, Léon. *Le célèbre Miracle de Saint Janvier a Naples et a Pouzzoles.* Paris: Gabriel Beauchesne, 1909. Impassioned argument that the "blood" attributed to St. Januarius behaves in a miraculous fashion.

Coulson, John, ed. *The Saints: A Concise Biographical Dictionary.* New York: Hawthorn, 1958: 238–39. A concise, rather skeptical treatment of the

Januarian "miracle."

Guerdon, David. "Le Sang de Saint Janvier se liquefie et se cogule depuis des siecles." *Psi International Bimestrial* 5 (1978): 9–29. Detailed and generally balanced treatment of all aspects of the Januarian phenomenon.

Rogo, D. Scott. *Miracles: A Parascientific Inquiry into Wondrous Phenomena.* New York: Dial, 1982: 186–202. A look at the "miracle" from a paranormalist's point of view.

Acknowledgments

We express our appreciation to the many who assisted us with this investigation over the years, including the late D. Scott Rogo, who graciously made available a translation of Guerdon (1978) that was of great value; Elizabeth Gregory, for help in translating from the French; Dr. Bernard J. Leikind, physicist, for reading and commenting on the manuscript; Dr. Robert A. Baker, for providing helpful published materials; and the staff of the Margaret I. King Library, University of Kentucky, for research assistance. We also wish to thank our Italian scientist friends, Luigi Garlaschelli, Franco Ramaccini, and Sergio Della Sala, not only for their own important research but also for the generous assistance they lent to our work.

10

Surviving a Fiery Fate
(Investigated with John F. Fischer)

The story of the man said to have survived a fiery fate—the legendary "hell's fire"—begins in the fall of 1974. At that time Jack B. Angel was a self-employed traveling salesman working out of College Park, Georgia. On or about the thirteenth of November, a Wednesday, he arrived at the Ramada Inn in Savannah where he was to meet a prospective buyer for the clothing he sold. Unfortunately, however, Angel was an hour late and missed the appointment with the client. Finding no room at the inn, he decided instead to spend the night in his converted motorhome—a sort of mobile showroom—in the Ramada parking lot.

The next day, apparently, Angel started to take a shower, but he was reportedly unable to account for his time after that. The next thing he recalls was awakening about noon the following day, November 15, and discovering he had inexplicably received several injuries, particularly one to his right hand. "It was just burned, blistered," Angel later stated.

"And I had this big explosion in my chest. It left a hell of a hole." Also, he recalled, he was burned in the groin area, and on the legs and back "in spots!"; yet neither his pajamas or bed sheets, nor anything else in the motorhome was singed! Physicians examining him, he insisted, "explained to me I wasn't burned externally; I was burned internally."[1]

Moreover, according to a brief report in the December 1981 *Omni,* the popular science magazine, Angel's Savannah physician specifically attributed the burns to "spontaneous combustion," described as "a bizarre molecular reaction . . . that causes people to burn up inside." The physician, Dr. David Fern, who had reportedly been summoned to the scene of Angel's accident, supposedly maintained there was no other reasonable explanation, since nearby objects in the mobile trailer showed no traces of fire damage.[2]

Actually, Dr. Fern had neither gone to the scene nor rushed to any such judgment. (Angel was first admitted to the Memorial Medical Center in Savannah, then was later transferred to a Veterans Administration hospital and the care of Dr. Fern.) While declining to make a determination of the exact cause, the physician did state:

> Mr. Angel presented himself to the hospital with a severe burn injury of the hand and *minor injury* of the chest wall. This was a third-degree burn which damaged the skin severely and most of the underlying muscle of the hand, causing a total anaesthetic hand. (Emphasis added.)

As a consequence, Angel's burned right hand had to be amputated. Dr. Fern later stated, "The description of the burn and the findings in surgery are very typical of an electric-type injury. This generates a high-powered heat source because of the resistance of the skin and the underlying tissue."[3]

But Larry Arnold, a Pennsylvania schoolbus driver who is an arch-advocate of the reality of spontaneous human combustion (SHC), asks: "Where—and what—could this predicted high-energy source be?" As he reported in his article, "The Man Who Survived Spontaneous Combustion" (in the September 1982 *Fate*), thorough investigation eliminated such external sources as power lines and lightning storms. Angel's lawyers (who had volunteered to represent him on a contingency-fee basis) next hired an engineering laboratory to inspect the motorhome's interior. "Electrical test instruments evaluated the vehicle's *Onan* generator and AC wiring and uncovered no problems," Arnold states. "Further inspection failed to locate discoloration or other physical evidence which might have been left by the heat that burned Angel's body."[4]

Finally, Arnold reports, the engineers "turned to the only remaining suspected source of heat in the vehicle: its hot-water plumbing system." However, although the Ramada Inn's maintenance man had thought the burns looked like those from scalding water, as from loosening a radiator cap, again there was, Arnold insisted, a lack of evidence. Not only was the radiator cap tightly in place, but there were also no ruptured pipes or other certain indication that hot water could have been the cause. There was, however, one clue: the hot water pump had a slipped drive belt. This led the engineers to theorize that, lacking hot water for a shower, Angel had gone outside, removed the heater's metal cover, and opened its safety valve. As a consequence, according to the engineer's theory, Angel was subjected to a blast of pressurized, scalding hot water.[5]

Arnold, however, could not accept such an explanation. He did not think a burn victim would have replaced the heater cover, and he concluded, based on the process of elimination, that "In this case the evidence points to the only remaining explanation: Spontaneous human combustion."

Conceding that the "scientific consensus" did not admit the existence of the alleged phenomenon, Arnold nevertheless concluded:

> The medical determination that burns were "internal" and the failure
> of precision engineering studies to provide a legally defensible external
> cause indicate that Jack Angel not only experienced SHC but—unlike
> the overwhelming majority of victims—survived to tell the tale.[6]

Arnold's approach is unfortunately all too common among researchers of the paranormal. Sensible explanations are frequently ruled out—

often by superficial, even slipshod investigation—whereas farfetched possibilities are stubbornly defended and attempts are made to shift the burden of proof. "Orthodox" scientists are disparaged for being too timid to accept that which is seen as a brave new vision, but so often turns out to be the merest mirage.

In the Angel case, for instance, Arnold accepts Angel's allegation that unnamed doctors told him his burns were "internal," even though Dr. Fern's description of the burns and his other statements indicate the injuries were consistent with an external source.

Such was the state of affairs when we became tacitly involved in the case in 1984. We had just published the results of our two-year investigation of SHC in the form of a lengthy report in the journal of the International Association of Arson Investigators.[7] Our study comprised thirty historic cases, spanning more than two-and-a-half centuries, that seemed representative of the supposed phenomenon but that turned out to have rational explanations. (See fig. 18.)

For example, there was the 1731 death of an Italian countess whose body was reportedly reduced to "a heap of ashes." Charles Dickens was among those who believed the case lent credence to the existence of SHC, and it served as a source for the gruesome spontaneous-combustion death that he portrayed in his novel *Bleak House.*

Investigation of that case, however, took us back to an account in a 1746 issue of *Gentlemen's Magazine.* As it related, on the floor of the countess's chamber was found an ash-covered lamp, empty of oil. This suggests that the unfortunate woman had fallen on the lamp and that the flowing oil had aided in the immolation.

In another case that transpired before 1835 (when it was published in Theodoric R. Beck and John B. Beck's *Elements of Medical Jurisprudence*), a thirty-year-old woman burned to death in New York. A hole four feet in diameter had burned through the floor of her room, leaving her remains on the ground below.

Again, however, investigation revealed the case to be less mysterious than SHC proponents would suggest. The woman, Hannah Bradshaw, had been intoxicated and, as indicated by a candlestick found near the edge of the hole, had probably set her clothes afire by brushing against the candle.

In more modern times there is the death of Mrs. Mary Reeser, who perished by fire in St. Petersburg, Florida, in 1951. Termed the "best documented modern case," it came under special scrutiny. We learned that when last seen Mrs. Reeser was sitting in an overstuffed chair, wearing flammable nightclothes, and smoking a cigarette—this after having taken sleeping pills!

Although it was true that Mrs. Reeser's body was severely destroyed while her efficiency apartment suffered relatively little damage, there were rational explanations for both facts. The floor and walls of the apartment were of concrete, which helped prevent the fire from spreading. Also, as indicated by "grease" found at the spot where the chair had stood, the plump widow's own fat had probably contributed to the destruction of her body. (In what is known in the forensic literature as the "candle effect," the melted body fat was apparently absorbed by the chair's stuffing, fueling the slow-burning fire that then destroyed more of the body while yielding yet more melted fat to continue the process.)

Still more recently, there was the 1966 death of Dr. J. Irving Bentley in Coudersport, Pennsylvania, a death Larry Arnold suggests was due to spontaneous human combustion. Actually, it is known that the ninety-two-year-old physician was a pipe smoker who frequently dropped smoldering ashes on his clothing. Burns on the bathroom floor suggested this had happened a final time, and Dr. Bentley had made his way with his aluminum walker to the bathroom where he vainly attempted to extinguish the flames. That he had shed his robe, found smoldering in the bathtub, demonstrated that the source of combustion was *external,* not internal as SHC proponents imagine.[8]

After our report was published, we received letters from some of our fellow "anomaly" researchers—notably Jerome Clark—raising the issue of the Angel case. One of us (J. N.) replied with a few casual observations based solely on Arnold's *Fate* article:

1. The case poorly compared to alleged SHC cases, in which the extremities were often spared but in which the burning—once begun—could scarcely be extinguished (even when water was poured on the body).

2. There was *directionality* implicit in the fact that the hand received the greatest damage, the chest less, and the groin and ankle, respectively, still less, suggesting (as the letter continued) "that [Angel's] hand contacted some potent, radiating energy source—possibly electrical or one spewing hot water.

3. There were "indications he was in a stupor after the accident" (for example, Angel told Arnold, "I was staggering like I was drunk"), and that it seemed "interesting that his first impulse was to visit a bar and order hard liquor," rather than seek medical assistance. (In other words, what if Angel had been in an earlier stupor—however induced—and that had helped *cause* an accident?)[9]

We did not immediately follow Clark's later suggestion that we actually investigate the Angel case (largely because we were swamped with work at the time), but we did privately discuss the case at some length. It seemed to us that the preponderance of evidence indicated hot water rather than electricity as the probable cause. Assuming it was true that Angel's pajamas were unscorched, and considering there was a lack of burn marks anywhere on the motorhome, electrical burning seemed quite unlikely; yet the facts would be fully consistent with scalding water. So would the appearance of the wounds—not, perhaps, the "charred" hand that Angel later described, but the description by Dr. Fern, as well as by the motel maintenance man. And there were other indications.

What we did not know was that another investigator had been pursuing the Angel case. Best known for his articles and books debunking UFO reports, Phil Klass had become intrigued by the matter and gone in search of an Unexplained Fiery Origin. He queried the lawyers involved, obtained a copy of the previously mentioned engineering report, and—most importantly—secured copies of the court records. He generously entrusted his entire investigative file on the case to us, allowing us to copy it and—for the first time—to make the findings public. It served as a basis for our own subsequent review-investigation of the Angel case.

As we discovered, contained in the 1975 civil-action suit filed by Angel's attorney in the Superior Court for Fulton County, Georgia, is the following account:

> On November 21 [sic], 1974, Plaintiff was attempting to take a shower in said motorhome which was parked on a motel parking lot in Savannah, Georgia. While Plaintiff was in the process of taking a shower, the water suddenly stopped flowing from the shower plumbing.
>
> Plaintiff, in attempting to discover the reason for the loss of water pressure, exited said motorhome and attempted to inspect the hot water heater. In making said inspection of the hot water heater, the pressure valve on the hot water heater released and as a result, scalding hot water under tremendous pressure was sprayed upon Plaintiff.

The complaint asserted that the defendant (the manufacturer of the motorhome) was negligent in failing to provide a safer design for the heater and pressure valve and also for failing to warn, either on the heater or in the instruction booklet, of the danger that might be encountered.[10] (The suit was later moved to federal court and subsequently dismissed for costs paid by the defendant.)[11]

Lest anyone attribute the foregoing narrative of events to the retrospective imagination of Angel or his legal counsel, there is further, corroborative evidence. First, there are the statements of a Mr. Ed Jonikens who had visited Angel in the hospital and then drove the salesman's vehicle home for him. He, too, thought Angel's injuries appeared to be the results of scalding. And, when he reached the motorhome, Jonikens found the panel on the water heater to be "extremely hot."[12]

Of even greater significance, the engineers who examined the motorhome had not only found that the water pump's drive belt was off (as Arnold reported), but they also discovered *the water heater's safety-relief valve was in the open position.*[13] This crucial fact was confirmed by a later engineering study commissioned by the motorhome corporation's insurance company.[14]

Therefore, the legal documents and the physical evidence at the scene of the injury, together with the medical findings and statements of involved persons, clearly establish that Jack Angel was accidentally self-injured by a scalding, pressurized jet from his motorhome's hot water system—*not* by "spontaneous human combustion," a phenomenon whose existence remains as doubtful as before.

In a subsequent letter to *Fate* magazine Larry Arnold took a defiant tone. Always referring to himself in the plural (i.e., as "we" and "us"), he discounted our claims of corroborative evidence and asserted: "We interviewed three recreational vehicle technicians/dealers who represent 36 years' experience servicing ARCO/RV water systems. They agreed that it was rare for such a valve to go bad, and the water would drain down, and not out, anyway."[15]

Despite our polite request,[16] Arnold refused to provide the names of his alleged—but anonymous—experts.[17] Thus we were unable to consult with them to see whether they had been fully apprised of the facts in the case.

Nevertheless, we wrote a response to Arnold's *Fate* letter, pointing out, first of all, that we had not postulated "a bad valve."[18] We also provided a numbered list of fifteen factors that corroborate the theory that Angel's burns were due to scalding. We think they are worth repeating here.

First, there were no fewer than eleven factors mentioned in our article:

1. The *open* safety valve.
2. The water pump's slipped drive belt.
3. The "extremely hot" heater panel.

4. The conclusion of engineers who examined the heating unit.
5. Inspection of the electrical system (ruling out an alternate source for the accident).
6. Absence of burn marks inside the motorhome.
7. Angel's unburned clothing (especially consistent with scalding).
8/9. Two early observers' descriptions of Angel's burns.
10. His physician's description of the burns (indicating an *external* source, whatever its identity).
11. The pattern of damage (greatest to the hand, progressively less to chest, groin, and ankle).

We also listed four additional corroborative factors (not mentioned in our article):

12. Burns on Angel's back, "in spots," consistent with spattering by hot water.
13. *Another* expert inspection, substantiating the basic findings of the one we cited.
14. A loose water-pump drive pulley (the obvious cause of the slipped drive belt).
15. A medical report quoting Angel as stating he ran out of hot water while taking a shower.

Still other factors could be mentioned, but surely those listed are sufficient for reasonable people to see how futile is the postulation of "spontaneous human combustion" as a source for Jack Angel's injuries. As in other cases of the alleged phenomena that we have investigated, a plausible, naturalistic cause was readily found. It is lamentable that proponents of SHC seem repeatedly unable to discover such evidence themselves, or to appreciate it once it is presented to them.

Notes

1. Quoted in Larry Arnold, "The Man Who Survived Spontaneous Combustion," *Fate,* Sept. 1982, 60–65.

2. Harry Lebelson, "Human Combustion" ("Anti-Matter" section), *Omni,* Dec. 1981, 133.

3. Quote in Arnold, "Man Who Survived Spontaneous Combustion," 62–63 and 65n.

4. Arnold, "Man Who Survived Spontaneous Combustion," 63–64.

5. Ibid., 64.

6. Ibid., 65.

7. Joe Nickell and John F. Fischer, "Spontaneous Human Combustion," *The Fire and Arson Investigator* 34, no. 3 (March 1984): 4–11; 34, no. 4 (June 1984): 3–8.

8. Ibid. These cases are also discussed in Joe Nickell with John F. Fischer, *Secrets of the Supernatural* (Buffalo, N.Y.: Prometheus Books, 1988), 149–57, 161–71.

9. Joe Nickell, letter to Jerome Clark, Nov. 11, 1984.

10. Civil Action File No. C-9540, Superior Court for Fulton County, Georgia, n.d.: amendment filed Sept. 23, 1975. (Note: The date given for the accident, November 21, is not supported by other documents—including two engineering reports—which give November 15. Arnold [n. 1] gives dates that are also at variance with the documents, with the result that he has Angel unconscious *for four days*—from November 12 to 16.)

11. Civil Action File No. C-75-2160 A, United States District Court, Northern District of Georgia, Atlanta Division, filed May 31, 1977.

12. Quoted in the engineering report commissioned by Angel's attorney, a copy of which, provided by Klass, is in our investigative file.

13. Ibid.

14. Report of Gottschalk Engineering Associates, Inc., Atlanta, Georgia, Aug. 19, 1975.

15. Larry Arnold, letter to editor, *Fate,* Sept. 1989, 125–26.

16. Joe Nickell, letter to Larry Arnold, Oct. 25, 1989.

17. Larry Arnold, letter to Joe Nickell, Nov. 1, 1989. I sent a further request to him on November 10 and received a further refusal on November 21: "We just don't see any benefits that would accrue by releasing this information

to you at this time."

18. Joe Nickell, letter to the editor, *Fate,* Dec. 1989, 126.

Select Bibliography

Arnold, Larry. "The Man Who Survived Spontaneous Combustion." *Fate,*
    September 1982: 60–65. An account of Jack Angel's burn injuries, and
    fanciful "theory" of their cause.

Gaddis, Vincent H. *Mysterious Fires and Lights.* New York: David McKay,
    1967. Pseudoscientific treatment of allegedly paranormal fiery phenomena.

Nickell, Joe, and John F. Fischer. "Did Jack Angel Survive Spontaneous
    Combustion?" *Fate,* May 1989: 80–84. An investigative report on the Angel
    case.

Nickell, Joe, with John F. Fischer. *Secrets of the Supernatural.* Buffalo, N.Y.:
    Prometheus Books, 1988. A casebook of the paranormal, including a chapter
    on the Mary Reeser "SHC" case and an appendix of thirty historic cases
    of the alleged phenomenon.

Acknowledgments

In an earlier, briefer form, this chapter appeared as "Did Jack Angel Survive
Spontaneous Combustion?" *Fate,* May 1989: 80–84. It is reprinted by permission.

11

The Crop-Circle Phenomenon
(Investigated with John F. Fischer)

For years a mysterious phenomenon has been plaguing southern English crop fields. Typically producing swirled, circular depressions in cereal crops, it has left in its wake beleaguered farmers and an astonished populace, not to mention befuddled scientists and would-be "investigators"—all struggling to keep apace of the proliferating occurrences and the equally proliferating claims made about them.

The Mystery and the Controversy

The circles range in diameter from as small as three meters (nearly ten feet across) to some twenty-five meters (approximately eighty-two feet) or more. In addition to the simple circles that were first reported, there have appeared circles in formations; circles with rings, spurs, and

177

other appurtenances; and yet more complex forms including "picto-graphs" and even a crop triangle! While the common depression or "lay" pattern is spiral (either clockwise or counterclockwise), there are radial and even more complex lays.[1]

Typically, the configurations crop up (so to speak) in fields of wheat, rye, barley, and other cereal crops—or "corn," as the British say. However, they have also been reported in soybeans, sugar beets, mustard, etc., as well as grass.[2]

The year 1989 brought no fewer than three books on the cornfield phenomenon and added to the already countless number of articles on the subject. Soon circles-mystery enthusiasts were being called cereol-ogists (after Ceres, the Roman goddess of vegetation). Circlemania was in full bloom.

By this time, some of the nascent explanations for the early, relatively simple circles had been debunked. The circles' matted pinwheel patterns readily distinguished them from fairy rings (rings of lush growth in lawns and meadows, caused by parasitic fungi).[3] The possibility that they were due to the sweeping movements of snared or tethered animals, or rutting deer, seemed precluded by the absence of any tracks or trails of bent or broken stems.[4] And the postulation of helicopters flying upside down was countered by the observation that such antics would produce, not swirled circles, but crashed 'copters.[5]

Nevertheless, the possibility that the circles were due to ordinary helicopter downwash invited a more serious response. As demonstrated on a BBC program, downdrafts actually spread and ripple over an area so that the grain stalks are pushed out, never producing sharply defined edges like those of the crop circles. Moreover, although it might seem logical that downwash would be spiral, given the rotary motion of helicopter blades, it is not, and it cannot create the swirl pattern that typifies most crop circles.[6]

A "scientific" explanation was soon attempted by George Terence Meaden, a one time professor of physics who later took up meteorology as an avocation. In 1974 he founded the Tornado and Storm Research Organization (known by the lively acronym TORRO). He soon revived the defunct magazine, *The Journal of Meteorology,* which increasingly became a forum for Meaden's views that the crop-circles phenomenon is an atmospheric one. In his book, *The Circles Effect and Its Mysteries,* he boasts: "Ultimately, it is going to be the theoretical atmospheric physicist who will successfully minister the full and correct answers."[7]

Meaden's notion is that the "circles effect" is produced by what he terms the "plasma vortex phenomenon." He defines this as "a spinning mass of air which has accumulated a significant fraction of electrically-charged matter." Most evidence, he contends, "suggests that the spinning wind has entered the ionized state known as plasma, and that the vortices are to become plasma balls akin to ball lightning in appearance except that they are much bigger and longer-lived." When the electrically charged, spinning mass strikes a crop field, Meaden thinks, it produces a neat crop circle.[8]

Variant forms, he contends, are also allowed by his postulated vortices. For example, of satellite circles, Meaden states: "An induction effect may be the consequence of electromagnetic-wave interference resulting in antimodal extrema at the satellite positions, thus leading to secondary rotating plasmas at these locations." Circle rings, which "quite often" rotate in a direction opposite to that of the inner circle, may be due to a "counter-rotating sheath," the reason for the existence of which, the theorist admits, "is obscure." Because of their capacity to be ionized, Meaden asserts, the vortices can produce light and sound effects that have been associated with the creation of some circles.[9]

However, as even one of Meaden's staunchest defenders concedes, "natural descending vortices . . . are as yet unrecognized by meteorologists."[10] Meaden himself acknowledges that "some from among my professional colleagues who have expressed surprise at the discovery of the circles effect and questioned why it has not previously attracted the attention of scientists, prefer to deny its existence and reject the entire affair as a skillful hoax." He huffs: "Attitudes of negation are ill-considered and counter-scientific; one recalls those blinkered academics of last century who refused to accept that meteorites could be extra-terrestrial despite the wealth of *prima facie* proof assembled in favour."[11]

(Of course, his skeptical colleagues might well counter with examples of those—including scientists—who rushed to ascribe new energy forces to phenomena now regarded as having more mundane explanations.)

In contrast to Meaden's approach is that of Pat Delgado and Colin Andrews, two engineers who have extensively studied and recorded the crop-circle phenomenon. Whereas Meaden attempts a "scientific" explanation, Delgado and Andrews seem primarily interested in presenting a mystery. Fascinated by the "detail within the rings and circles," as they say in their first book, *Circular Evidence* (1989), they portray it as "a mystery within a mystery." Not surprisingly, they therefore disparage "those who debunk the unknown," and they are quick—too quick, it seems—to dismiss the possibility that the geometric designs are the work of hoaxers.[12]

The pages of *Circular Evidence* are filled with digressions and irrelevancies—all calculated to foster mystery. For example, we learn of the authors' meeting with a professor and a member of the British Psychical Research Society, "a meeting," say the authors knowingly, "which we recorded although the tape was blank when we played it back." A dog that became ill at one site, "some kind of magnetic disturbance" at another, and a plane that crashed after flying over a field where crop circles had appeared some eight weeks before—these are the apparently random occurences that Delgado and Andrews attempt to yoke into the mystery.[13]

Overall, Delgado and Andrews hint most strongly at the UFO hypothesis—perhaps not surprisingly since both have been consultants to *Flying Saucer Review*.[14] Although they profess "guarded views" about whether circles and rings have an extraterrestrial source, they frequently give the opposite impression. For example they go out of their way to observe that a 1976 circle "appeared about seven weeks before a Mrs. [Joyce] Bowles had seen a UFO [and a silver-suited humanoid] just down the road." Again, after visiting one circle Andrews met two teenagers, one of whom had earlier seen "an orange glowing object" nearby.[15] Other mysterious lights and objects are frequently alluded to, and the cereologists conclude:

Each new formation strengthens the current feeling of many people that we are dealing with something which hints at some form of manipulated force. Nothing in the current state of conventional science can account for all that has been described in this book.[16]

But is everything so described accurately represented? Is the evidence against hoaxing (to be discussed presently) really so strong as the cereologists proclaim? Are we to factor in all the little nonmysteries? Are we really to take seriously even the antics of dowsing rods and pendulums—utilized by Delgado and Andrews, as well as by Meaden, to detect circle "energies"?[17]

Then there is the reliance on anecdotal evidence (i.e., evidence in the form of personal stories, such as the "eyewitness" tales that supposedly proved Elvis Presley still lives). In this respect, it seems that both Meaden and the Delgado and Andrews team have much in common. For example, Meaden offers three alleged eyewitnesses to the vortex creation of a circle (a surprisingly small number, given the frequency of the phenomenon, and one was an associate of Meaden). Unfortunately, all waited several years before making their claims, and none described the respective events in quite the same way.[18] Similarly, Delgado and Andrews associate UFO sightings with circle formation, such as the night "a row of bright lights" was seen at the famous Devil's Punch Bowl at Cheesefoot Head, Hampshire.[19] Use of such conflicting anecdotal evidence has prompted one writer to state rather cynically:

As long as the phenomenon continues, time is on the side of the believers, of course. More and more witnesses, with tales that conform to the dominant myth, will certainly come forward. The witness battalion has already grown since the books appeared.[20]

Almost predictably, a *hybrid* of the main theories has appeared in "eyewitness" form. Late one evening in early August 1989, or so they claimed, two young men witnessed a circle being formed near Margate, Kent. One of them, a nineteen-year-old, described "a spiralling vortex of flashing light" (a nod to Meaden et al.) that, however, "looked like an upturned satellite TV dish with lots of flashing lights" (a sop to flying saucer theorists). The youth kept a straight face while posing for a news photo with the circle.[21]

As the crop-circle phenomenon entered the decade of the nineties, bringing with it the emergence of ever more complex forms that earned the sobriquet "pictograms," the main circular theorists rushed into print their various "Son of Crop Circles" sequels. Delgado and Andrews rang in with their *Crop Circles: The Latest Evidence* and Meaden with *Circles from the Sky* (a co-edited hardcover edition of a conference proceedings). Paul Fuller and Jenny Randles (who are Meaden's disciples although, ironically, they are UFOlogists) followed their *The Controversy of the Circles* with *Crop Circles: A Mystery Solved,* and Ralph Noyes edited a collection of writings on the topic titled *The Crop Circle Enigma.* Several periodicals also sprang up, devoted to the phenomenon and bearing names like *The Cereologist, The Crop Watcher,* and *The Circular.*[22] (*The Circular* is published by the Centre for Crop Circle Studies, whose "President and Director of Research" is a Prof. George Wingfield. Wingfield sees religious symbolism in the circles, and he advocates dowsing and "channeling"—the use of trance mediums—to provide "evidence" of authenticity.)[23]

If critics of the main theories were not capitalizing on an expanding market of interest in crop circles, they were nevertheless busily poring over the data and pointing out that the prevailing circle theories were, well, full of holes. We were among them.

Data Analyses

Our interest in the swirled-crops phenomenon increased during the latter 1980s. We had already opened a file on the subject, but now we sought to gather information (an important first stage of an investigation) at an accelerated pace. Rather than merely file the occasional article or set of notes, we began to gather data voraciously. We ordered books, corresponded with others who might offer input, monitored (or had monitored on our behalf) various periodicals and electronic mail networks, tapped the case file of the Committee for the Scientific Investigation of Claims of the Paranormal (CSICOP), obtained copies of documentary films, queried those who had experienced the phenomenon, etc., etc.

As we studied the incoming data and photographs, we began to formulate hypotheses and to seek out the opinions of agronomists and others who might be helpful. We also enlisted the aid of a computer expert to help us compile and analyze data on the swirled-crops phenomenon—a phenomenon we naturally distinguish from the simple circles or rings that, as everyone knows, may result from a number of causes.[24]

It soon struck us, as we came to learn that it had many other observers, that the crop-circle phenomenon had a number of potentially revealing characteristics. Cereologists—whether of the "scientific" or "paranormal" stripe—tend either to deny these characteristics or to posit alternate explanations for them. For the implications are serious: While any *single* attribute may be insufficient to identify a phenomenon, since other phenomena may share that feature, sufficient *multiple* qualities may allow one to rule certain hypotheses in or out so as to make an identification.

The phenomenon we allude to is hoaxing, and the characteristics that point to it include an escalation in frequency, the geographic distribution, an increase in complexity over time, and what we call the "shyness effect"—as well as a number of lesser features.

THE ESCALATION IN FREQUENCY

This aspect of the phenomenon has been well reported. Although there have been reports of circles and rings in earlier years and in various countries, e.g., circles of reeds in Australia in 1966 and a burned circle of grass in Connecticut in 1970, only a few had the flattened swirl feature, and few of those were well documented at the time.[25]

In any case, by the mid-1970s, what are now regarded as "classic" crop circles had begun to appear. In 1976, swirled circles in tall grass were shown near a Swiss village by a man who claimed he was regularly visited by extraterrestrials.[26] Delgado and Andrews report an anecdotal instance in England that same year and provide a farmer's photo from 1978 depicting part of a large swirled circle. (There were reportedly four smaller circles spaced evenly around it.) Meaden was drawn to the phenomenon in 1980;[27] Delgado saw his first circles in 1981. Delgado's response was "to share the experience with other people, so I contacted several national papers, along with the BBC and ITN." Then, he says, "Local papers jumped on the bandwagon as soon as they could get the story in print."[28] Delgado's use of the word "bandwagon" seems appropriate, since the term refers to an increasingly popular trend or fad. According to Ralph Noyes in an article titled "Circular Arguments," the crop-circles phenomenon "gives the appearance of elaborating and increasing its intrusions from year to year." Writing in 1989, he said that year had "brought more occurrences than ever before."[29] He is echoed by John Michell who wonders what force is creating the circles, stating: "The question becomes more urgent every year as the circles increase in number, size and variety."[30]

In an attempt to quantify and assess such perceptions we decided to data-bank information on the circles. We used the data in Delgado and Andrews's *Circular Evidence,* which reviewers praised over Meaden's and Fuller and Randles's books for its "level of detail"[31] and being "more comprehensive."[32] "Over the years," John Michell says of Delgado and Andrews, "they have inspected, measured, photographed, mapped and annotated hundreds of circles."[33] Of course we considered that the incidences of the phenomenon in their book did not represent a complete list, but we intended to look at other sources of data as a cross-check on the sample.

With these caveats in mind we gave a copy of *Circular Evidence* to computer expert Dennis Pearce, an advisory engineer with Lexmark International. Plotting the number of circles per year, Pearce determined, showed a definite (i.e., significantly greater than exponential) increase in the number of crop circles annually from 1981 to 1987.[34]

This was well supported by data from Meaden's article, "A Note on Observed Frequencies of Occurrence of Circles in British Cornfields," in *Fortean Times*. Figures for the four years from 1980–1983 were, respectively, 3, 3, 5, and 22; Meaden does not give exact figures for the next few years, but notes they were "rising." Then during the 1987–1989 the totals went from 73 to 113 to "over 250" annually.[35] For 1990, the figure had again jumped remarkably—to 700 circles in Britain, at least according to Randles.[36] Small wonder that even moderate voices in the controversy, like Noyes and Michell, insist the phenomenon is increasing.

Meaden and his followers, however, do not accept that there has actually been such a marked increase over the decade. Meaden attributes the increase in part to aerial surveillance begun in 1985. "In addition," he says, "totals for earlier years were still rising, partly as a result of feedback from helpful farmers who were telling us of occurrences of circles on their land which they had known about when they were young."[37]

But such anecdotal reports are untrustworthy in the extreme for reasons we have already considered, not the least of which is that we cannot at such a remove distinguish the "classic" phenomenon from other circles and rings. There are a number of circular formations that can occur in English fields, such as the outlines of flattened prehistoric burial mounds that can often be seen in aerial photos, that could easily be confused with crop circles. One farmer mentioned circles that regularly appeared in his fields during dry spells, but when taken to see a crop ring stated: "This isn't what I thought you meant. . . . I've never seen anything like this before."[38]

Meaden even mentions an instance that supposedly occured in 1678! Widely cited, it is the folk account of an alleged instance of witchcraft in Hertfordshire. Unfortunately for cereologists, the account specifically states that the oats were *cut*, not bent down in a swirled pattern like the crop circles.[39] Indeed, not only does this story of "The Mowing Devil" fail to support an early historical existence for crop circles, but, says one critic: "The phenomenon's general, if not total, lack of historical precedent is to me its most disturbing aspect."[40]

Jenny Randles largely agrees with Meaden, although she now increasingly allows for a great number of hoaxes. Speaking of the proliferation of circles that occurred in 1989 and 1990, she states:

> Both those years are hopelessly tainted by the social factors [i.e., the bandwagon effect we mentioned earlier] generated from the huge media hype. Before 1989 we were getting maybe 30 press stories a summer on circles. In 1989 we got up to 300 and in 1990 we had almost 1000. We can show that this escalation in publicity *preceded* the increase in circle totals and to us this strongly implies a correlation.

In short, she says, the number of circles has been swelled, "heavily contaminated by mass hoaxing inspired by all the publicity."[41]

Here Randles is helping skeptics make their case, because if there is indeed "mass hoaxing" might not the entire phenomenon be similarly caused? We agree with Randles that the escalation of the phenomenon seems to correlate with media coverage of it, and that the coverage helped prompt further hoaxes. We provided Dennis Pearce with statistics on crop-circle articles that appeared in *The Times* of London from 1986–1990, and he specially commented on "the rapid rise in both locations and number of circles in the years following the London *Times* reports," which, he said, "is to me evidence of human intervention."[42]

GEOGRAPHIC DISTRIBUTION

A second observed feature of the patterned-crops phenomenon is its predilection for a limited geographic area. As we have seen, prior to the mid-1970s crop circles appeared sporadically at scattered locations in various countries, but since then they have flourished in southern England—in Hampshire, Wiltshire, and nearby counties.

There it was that the circles effect captured the world's attention. In plotting the occurrences of formations among English counties, Pearce confesses himself "surprised at how localized the phenomenon is."[43]

Although there are known exceptions, such as an occurrence in adjacent Wiltshire in 1980, all the pre-1986 cases published by Delgado and Andrews in *Circular Evidence* were in Hampshire, with the vast majority remaining there during the period surveyed.[44]

Other sources provide additional evidence for the geographic preference. In 1989 *Time* magazine concluded: "while there have been reports of circles from as far away as the Soviet Union, Japan and New Zealand, by far the greatest number have appeared in Hampshire and Wiltshire."[45] The Associated Press, citing a total of 270 circles for the summer of 1989, reported that "two-thirds appeared in a square-mile zone near Avebury in Wiltshire's rural terrain, including 28 in one field."[46] And cereologist Terence Meaden reported an even greater concentration, stating, "Although circles were found in as many as 18 counties this year (1989), at least 210 of these were found in just one county, Wiltshire, in central southern England."[47]

Jenny Randles and Paul Fuller argue that, to the contrary, "sensible circle researchers have known for some years that circles appear all over Britain, but for various reasons formations appearing away from this area receive little publicity and go unreported outside their local media."[48] However, as Ralph Noyes counters, many of the reports Randles and Fuller cite are "poorly documented"; he adds that "If credit is given to them all, however, there still remains a strong appearance of an overwhelming concentration of events in Wessex [an area in southern England, after the name of the old Anglo-Saxon kingdom] and of a phenomenon which has developed explosively in the 1980's."[49] In fact, Randles and Fuller reproduce a chart from Meaden, "The geographical distribution of British circle sites," that shows a preponderance of circles in the southern half of England and a dense clustering of them in the Wessex area.[50] It is apparent that if Meaden's anecdotal reports were disallowed, the extent of the clustering would be even more dramatic.

It may not be coincidence, given the early sporadic circles' association with UFOs, that the clustering occurs where it does. The Wiltshire town of Warminster is "the famous UFO capital of England";[51] during the sixties and seventies it was what Randles and Fuller term "the centre of the UFO universe, drawing spotters from all over the world."[52] Therefore, the area may have provided a unique climate for hoaxes in the form of UFO landing sites (as the early Wessex circles were often thought to be) to flourish.

Some cereologists suggest that, within the densely circle-pocked area, the configurations do have a pecularity of distribution. Wind-vortex theorists, like Meaden and Fuller, insist that a high proportion of crop circles—some 50 percent—appear at the base of hills, a fact they attribute to the topography transforming air currents into vortices.[53] However, Delgado and Andrews observe that the circles form in a variety of locations—"many . . . remote from any hills"[54]—and skeptics are quick to point out that hills offer good vantage points from which hoaxers can view their creations.[55]

Looking beyond the Wessex area, just as the popular media's increasing reportage of the cornfield phenomenon appears to have produced an increase in circle totals—as even Jenny Randles concedes— it also correlates well with the spread of the phenomenon elsewhere. Looking at just the data in *Circular Evidence,* Dennis Pearce observed that the number of reported geographical locations in England per year grew at a faster-than-exponential rate. "I would suspect," he said, "that a natural phenomenon would be either consistently localized or consistently spread about, but not spreading rapidly over time."[56] Also, whereas the circles effect's pre-English distribution was exceedingly sparse, after newspaper and television reports on the phenomenon began to increase in the late eighties, circles began to crop up in significant numbers around the world. For example, in September 1990 two circles appeared in a Missouri sorghum field and were immediately followed by reports of circles in three other fields, one in Missouri and two in Kansas.[57]

About this time they had also begun to appear in significant numbers in Japan and Canada. Although circles had been reported sporadically in Canada since the mid-1970s, they reappeared with a vengeance in the fall of 1990. Soon after circles turned up in Manitoba in August, the *Toronto Globe and Mail* reported they were "appearing almost weekly now across the Prairies."[58] One of us (J. N.) was a guest on a radio program with a Saskatchewan farmer who was mystified by the appearance of the phenomenon in his wheat fields.[59] Perhaps inevitably, with the spread of circles came attendant reports of hoaxes.[60]

INCREASE IN COMPLEXITY

A third characteristic of the patterned-crops phenomenon is the tendency of the configurations to become increasingly elaborate over time. Looking first just at the data in *Circular Evidence,* we see a definite trend. The reports begin in 1978 with simple swirled circles (albeit circles in formation), then include circles with a single ring (July 1986), a circle with ring and satellite circles (August 1986), a circle with ring and arrow (September 1986), a double-ringed circle (1987), and so on,[61] including three circles in a "triangle" formation (1988) that was described as "a new phenomenon."[62]

Delgado and Andrews themselves state: "Before the late 1970s it looked as though single circles were all we had to consider; but, as has always been the pattern, and as we have learnt over the years, something, maybe some intelligent level, keeps one or more jumps ahead."[63] Again they say: "As soon as we think we have solved one peculiarity, the next circle displays an inexplicable variation, as if to say, 'what do you make of it now?' "[64]

A case in point involves Terence Meaden. When he first published *The Circles Effect and Its Mysteries* in mid-June 1989, setting forth his wind-vortex theory, he declared that "single rings around single circles always rotate in a sense opposite to that of the interior," and he explained that this was necessarily the case.[65] However, as John Michell writes:

> At the very same time that his book was published, on the morning of 18 June, a new type of circle appeared at Cheesefoot Head. It was in the familiar form of a ring around a circle, but it was different from all the others, for the corn [grain] in both its ring and its circle were swirled in the same direction.[66]

Meaden does acknowledge the seeming increase in complexity when he mentions that "plain single circles" were "the only ones known at the beginning."[67] However, even with the astonishing escalation in complexity that came in 1989 "when," says Randles, "a few highly complex patterns appeared," and in 1990 when the so-called "pictograms" sprang up,[68] Meaden has clung stubbornly to his vortex theory. He merely acknowledges "the amazing discoveries of recent years" and speaks of the "difficulties of interpretation," adding:

> As to the so-called "evolution" of circle-patterns, I believe that this is scarcely more than the result of chance discovery of whatever patterns happen to be present in a given year. There may be hundreds of different patterns, and each year we are treated to just a few of these depending on atmospheric and environmental conditions. In 1980 we knew only of single circles, in 1981 the first triple was seen, in 1983 the first quintuplets, in 1986 the first single-ringed circles, in 1987 the first double-ringed circle, and so on. But retrospective research was turning up pre-1980 evidence for some of these same formations. We learnt of a 1978 quintuplet from Hampshire (complete with photographs); and of certain pre-1980 ringed circles from other countries, we even know of a "doughnut" circle with dot centre for 1980.

Thus Meaden concludes:

> Much of the supposed "evolution" of the phenomenon—to which some have even ascribed "intelligence"—can therefore be explained rationally by an insufficiency of data. The more complete the archive becomes, the better this will be appreciated.[69]

To a degree, Meaden is correct; there were some moderately complex forms in earlier periods. (We previously mentioned circles in formations discovered in 1978, for example.) but the overall evolution of forms *within the Wessex area* still seems well established, and worldwide the emergence of the pictograms in 1990 clearly represented a new phase. States Meaden: "Admittedly, 1990 does look to be exceptional, but just because the reasons for this wait to be clarified, it would be fatuous to decree [that] an alien intelligence is at hand."[70]

The pictograms are wildly elaborate forms with a distinctly pictorial appearance. (See figs. 19 and 20.) There had been circles with key shapes and clawlike patterns; complex designs, consisting of circles and rings linked by straight bars and having various appendages and other stylized features; and still other configurations, including free-form "tadpole" shapes and even a crop *triangle*.[71] Small wonder that Delgado and Andrews, as well as others, suspect that the force that is making the designs is being "intelligently manipulated."[72]

During a Denver radio debate with one of us (J. N.), Delgado enthused about the phenomenon entering this new pictographic stage, earning the response that whereas he would probably be impressed if a crop picture of Mickey Mouse appeared, the ever-more-elaborate nature of the phenomenon suggested it was time to reconsider the hoax hypothesis.[73]

But few would have underestimated Delgado's will to believe had they known of the crop-*message* incident of 1987. The message, written in the typical flattened-crops style and with the words all run together, read: "WEARENOTALONE." Delgado told readers of *Flying Saucer Review:* "At first sight it was an obvious hoax, but prolonged study makes me wonder." Of the crop circles, he said: "Maybe these circles are created by alien beings using a force-field unknown to us. They may be manipulating existing Earth energy."[74]

Or the beings may be terrestrial ones, laboring by the sweat of their brows. At least the pictograms enabled Jenny Randles to wake up to the unmistakable evidence that hoaxes were not only occurring but were running rampant. She has admitted:

I do not believe that wind vortices created the pictograms, though serious research into that possibility continues. I know I differ here in my evaluation from both Terence Meaden and BUFORA [British UFO Research Association] colleague Paul Fuller. But saying this in no way compromises my views on the solution to other evidence. . . . I can think of very good reasons why the pictograms might well be expected, based on our sure knowledge that crop-circle hoaxing has greatly increased from just a few known cases before 1989 to a far higher figure deduced from my own personal site investigations in 1990. I would put the hoaxes to comprise something over 50 percent of the total.[75]

Fifty percent! Perhaps eventually she will revise that estimate upward, but in the meantime she has shown herself capable of a degree of skepticism. As she states: "Any researcher who does not anticipate that the enormous media interest in circles and the ease with which they can be faked would not lead to this escalation of contamination is foolish or wildly optimistic."[76]

We agree, except for the part about "contamination." Randles still believes that beyond the hoaxes is a genuine, wind-vortex-caused phenomenon, whereas there seems no need to postulate such. If the "experts" like Meaden, Delgado, and Andrews cannot tell the genuine crop circles from hoaxed ones in 50 percent of the cases, one wonders just of what the other 50 percent consists.

Two other aspects of the patterns' complexity are revealing. The first concerns the lay patterns that, like the configurations themselves, evolved in complexity. Whereas "The swirl lays of previous years had been orderly and depressed neatly," says Delgado and Andrews, 1987 produced more diverse and far more complex lay patterns.[77] They were even more elaborate in 1989. For example, the last circle of that year was termed a "masterpiece of nature," having a central swirled area and the remainder divided into quadrants; each segment showed "unbelievably perfect combing" with the grain stems in one quadrant aligned at right angles to those of the adjacent one, and so on around.[78]

Then there are the crop designs that have been formed in *stages,* not as single vortex strikes or other brief events. For example in 1987, report Delgado and Andrews, a month after a five-meter circle appeared, a larger, fifteen-meter circle "had superimposed itself" over it.[79] As another instance, a giant three-ringed circle with satellites photographed on May

19, 1990, was photographed again on May 27, whereupon it had developed an additional outer ring and ten more satellites.[80] Surely such work-in-progress seems like nothing so much as the effort of industrious hoaxers.

THE SHYNESS FACTOR

A fourth characteristic of the patterned-crops phenomenon is its avoidance of being observed in action. There is considerable evidence of this fact.

First of all there is its nocturnal aspect. Delgado and Andrews, who appear to have done the most extensive documentation of the phenomenon, state: "After extensive enquiry and prolonged personal observation, we have no evidence that these circles are created except at night."[81] After citing one such nocturnal event, they state:

> Many other confirmations of night-time creations come from farmers and people living near circle sites. "It wasn't there last night, but I noticed it first thing this morning," has become almost a stock statement. The evidence is overwhelming that circle creations only occur at night.[82]

Randles and Fuller agree that "most seem to form during the night or in daylight hours around dawn," adding,

> The nocturnal appearance of the majority of circles *might* suggest that hoaxing could be a plausible explanation for the phenomenon, because hoaxers would be expected to carry out their dubious activities under cover of darkness to escape detection and prosecution.[83]

However, they insist that "several circles are known to have appeared during daylight,"[84] although they do not explain. If they are referring to the alleged eyewitness accounts of vortex-formed circles, or other anecdotal evidence, they simply fail to make a case.

Besides, this concession that the circles phenomenon is *largely* nocturnal is important since that characteristic seems to run counter to the wind-vortex theory. In any case, whether or not one can say that *all* of the mysterious circles appear at night, one farmer explains: "Nobody ever sees them formed; we usually come across them when we are working in the fields."[85]

Not only does the circle-forming mechanism seem to prefer the dark, but it appears specifically to resist being seen, as shown by Colin Andrews's Operation White Crow. This was an eight-night vigil maintained by about sixty cereologists at Cheesefoot Head (a prime circles location) beginning June 12, 1989. Not only did the phenomenon fail to manifest itself in the field under surveillance, but also—although there had already been almost a hundred formations that summer, with yet another 170 or so to occur—*not a single circle was reported for the eight-day period anywhere in England!* Then a large circle and ring (the very set that, being swirled in the same direction, seem to play a joke on Meaden by upsetting his hypothesis) was discovered about 500 yards away *on the very next day!*[86]

The following year, the cereologists attempted to profit from their mistakes. This time they conducted a "top secret operation" termed Operation Blackbird that lasted three weeks beginning on July 23. They took two million dollars worth of technical equipment—including infra-red night-viewing camera equipment—to an isolated site where they maintained a nighttime vigil. Reuters quoted the irrepressible Colin Andrews as explaining what happened:

> "We had a situation at approximately 3:30 this morning on monitor—
> a number of orange lights taking the approximate form of a triangle
> and within that triangular form was a second triangle," Andrews said.
> "We had many lights, following that a whole complex arrangement
> of lights doing all sorts of funny things. It's a complex situation, we
> are actually analyzing it at this very moment. But there is undoubtedly
> something here for science."[87]

Pressed by reporters, Andrews denied that his group could have been fooled by a hoax.

Unfortunately for the credulous cereologists, Operation Blackbird turned out to be Situation Redface. When they and reporters converged on the site they discovered a hastily flattened set of six circles, together with some signs of the mysterious force that had created them: a wooden cross and a Ouija board placed at the center of each. Apparently the bobbing lights that had been seen were due to the infrared monitoring of the pranksters' body heat. Huffed an embarrassed Andrews: "It was only funny for about ten seconds. Otherwise it was totally irresponsible and set back serious research considerably."[88] At least the event under-scored an earlier statement by Andrews: "We now have the data to prove these circles are intelligently locating themselves."[89]

OTHER CHARACTERISTICS

Additional features of the "circles effect" are varied and revealing. Although Ralph Noyes insists that "Hoax, as a general theory can be consigned to the dustbin of 'explanation im,' " he notes an interesting apparent characteristic of the phenomenon. This is the way an elaborat' feature, the segmented–lay pattern referred to earlier, seemed to have been anticipated a few weeks before. In a nearby field had appeared, says Noyes aptly, "what seems to be the first rough sketch of it." He asks: "was something *practicing* on that earlier occasion?"[90]

The "something" apparently uses a variety of techniques in doing its sketching and drawing. This is evident not only in the general variety of lay patterns (swirl, radial, etc.), but also in specific details. For exam-ple, Delgado and Andrews explain that one circle "looks as though the floor was first swept around counter-clockwise, then the edge was finished off with a thin circular stroke in the opposite direction."[91] Another circle is notable for "serration marks" found on a few stems and leaves; another shows a tightly wound center (as if the stems were wound about a post that was then removed); and so on.[92]

We have already indicated the phenomenon's seeming propensity for mischief. As cereologist Archie E. Roy states: "The phenomenon begins to have the look of a large-scale jokester who is leading us by the nose."[93] John Michell mentions the "perversity" of the phenomenon in producing new patterns that invalidate previous hypotheses.[94] And Hilary Evans observes that "whoever/whatever is responsible for the crop circles shows every sign of playing games with us."[95]

Among the characteristics of the phenomenon are its generally abrupt edges and its elaborately stylized forms. As Randles and Fuller concede (although making a dubious analogy to snowflakes): "These patterns *look* disturbingly artificial.[96]

Additional characteristics are summed up by Noyes:

> The facts—the sheer brute history of this subject—suggest that we have an agency at work which exhibits a degree of skill, an agency which makes a preliminary sketch, pauses a while to take stock of its handiwork, and then goes on to complete the polished version. An agency which, after a while grows bored with what it is doing. . . . And doesn't do it again, except perhaps to keep its hand in. . . . And then stretches its imagination further.[97]

The Hoax Hypothesis

We believe that, taken together, the characteristics we have described—the escalation in frequency, the geographic distribution, the increase in complexity, the "shyness effect," and other features—are entirely consistent with the work of hoaxers.

That there *are* hoaxed crop circles no one can deny; the question is of the extent of the hoaxing, that is, whether, if all the hoaxes are eliminated, there would still be a residue of genuine circles that would require postulating some hitherto unproven phenomenon, such as wind vortexes or extraterrestrial visitations.

We have seen that some of the cereologists' evidence—the alleged eyewitness accounts, the supposed correlation of circle sites with hilly terrain, and some other claims—are at best unproved and unconvincing. But there are additional assertions.

One is that tests of grain from crop circles showed a significant difference in "energy levels" from that in non–crop-circle areas. In fact, a prominent cereologist, the Earl of Haddington, submitted "blind" samples for testing to the Spagyrik Laboratory after receiving confirmation from its director that it could indeed detect the different "energy levels." But in *The Cereologist* Haddington reported: "Days, weeks passed, months passed, with phone calls at regular intervals always given the same reply. We will put it [the report of the results] in the post tomorrow." After six months Haddington concluded: "When they are not told which sample came from a Crop Circle and which from a heap of grain in my back yard they are either unable or unwilling to give a result."[98] (Other claims of differences in "energy levels" come from the many cereologists who employ dowsing or "witching" wands and pendulums to detect the mystical forces. Needless to say, such claims remain unproven.)[99]

Many alleged characteristics of the circles are disputed. Is the phenomenon "silent" as some claim, or is it sometimes accompanied by a "humming or chirping" sound that does not appear to be very consistent and might be almost anything? Again, consider the row of "detached" and "dancing" lights that were seen on the same night a circle was formed: did they indeed represent a UFO "above the trees" or could they have been a line of hoaxers with flashlights on a distant slope?[100]

If the cereologists cannot offer much in the way of positive evidence, they nevertheless make several negative claims, notably that hoaxers cannot produce circles with the qualities of the "genuine" ones. But what are these qualities? In the debate with Delgado on the Denver radio program, it was difficult to get a straight answer from him on this issue.

His main argument was the alleged lack of broken-stemmed plants in the "genuine" formations, a point he and Andrews make repeatedly in *Circular Evidence*. For example, they say of one circle that "The root end of each stem is bent over and pressed down hard with no damage to the plants, which is why they continued to grow and ripen horizontally."[101]

In response, his various equivocations were pointed out: e.g., in one instance "most" of the plants were undamaged (or rather unbroken; some had "serration" marks on them!). His contradictions were also noted: for instance, Andrews states of one crop ring that "Between the two radial splays was a line of buckled plants. Each one was broken at the knuckle along its stem length." Did he regard the formation as a hoax? No, he only said, as mysteriously as possible, "These collapsed plants appeared to have suffered whiplash damage, possibly caused by opposing forces meeting."[102] In other words, if the plants are unbroken, that is a mystery; if broken, that is another mystery.

It is entirely possible that the circles with broken plants are merely the less skillfully hoaxed ones. We also considered that the moistening effect of dew on plants bent at night might mitigate against breakage, while agronomists we talked with pointed out that from mid-May to early August the English wheat was green and could easily be bent over without breaking—indeed could only be broken with difficulty.[103]

Another supposed impossibility is for hoaxers to produce circles without leaving tracks, there allegedly being none in the case of "genuine" circles. But a study of numerous crop-circle photographs in the various publications reveals that virtually every circle would have been accessibly by the tractor "tramlines" that mark the fields in closely spaced, parallel rows. When cereologist George Wingfield showed slides at a Mutual UFO Network (MUFON) meeting, a skeptic observed "that only one photo was shown of the circles laying in a field without tractor ruts, and even then two clear walkways into the pattern were visible despite the oblique angle of Wingfield's photo."[104] In any case, one can carefully pick one's way through a field without leaving apparent tracks.[105]

Can cereologists really tell a hoaxed circle from a "genuine" one? Randles and Fuller provide a chart of features that supposedly differentiate one from the other.[106] But Randles's belief that the pictograms are not authentic, when Fuller and others think otherwise, suggests that there is little objective basis for making a judgment. Says Dennis Stacy, writing in the *MUFON UFO Journal*, "Most times, we're simply left to take the investigators' word for it, as if some sort of inherited sixth sense were at work."[107]

In fact, rushing to judgment seems a habit of certain cereologists. When ninety-eight circles appeared atop two hills in Wales in less than a week, Colin Andrews was described as spokesman for a "team of top scientists" who were going to investigate. Andrews asserted, "We believe we have something of major proportions. . . . Because of the scale of the formations, we are sure there is no human involvement." Alas, a follow-up report stated: "Red-faced scientists who investigated the 98 mystery circles in the Black Mountains of Wales have discovered they were made by a local farmer—to encourage grouse to settle."[108]

In what amounted to a test of his ability, Colin Andrews was asked by a BBC film crew to examine a circle they said they had found. Reportedly, upon visiting the pattern Andrews declared it genuine, but when the BBC explained that it was a hoaxed circle made especially for the occasion, Andrews decided that the circle looked "too perfect" to be genuine after all.[109]

In several cases hoaxers have come forth and confessed, although often the reaction of cereologists is to doubt them.[110] But Jenny Randles and Paul Fuller give credence to the claim of four farmhands from Cornwall that they had created the second 1986 circle-and-ring formation at Cheesefoot Head—one accepted as genuine by Delgado and Andrews. As Randles and Fuller state:

> We believe that the Cornishmen's claim may well be true. If it is, they hoaxed a convincing circle-and-ring formation in less than twenty minutes, right next to a major road, on a pleasant summer Sunday evening and without being caught in the act. . . . In fact, at least one leading researcher was quoted as suggesting that these circles were seemingly "perfect" and so could not be part of some hoax.[111]

Since we do not have definite knowledge of how particular "genuine" circles are made, the claim that hoaxers cannot have made them is a logical fallacy known as an argument *ad ignorantiam,* i.e., literally arguing from ignorance. As some observers point out, it is now clear that crop circles are comparatively easy to hoax.[112] In fact, the different lay patterns and other details discussed earlier suggest there are various ways of making circles, and indeed various techniques have been described in newspaper articles and books and even detailed by the hoaxers themselves.

The Cornish farmhands explained that they produced their circle "by shuffling along on our knees to push down the wheat, then rolling around our bodies in a complete circle."[113] Two farmers at Westbury, Wiltshire, produced a quintuplet formation on their own land using a pole and chain.[114] And so on.

An effective method was filmed by the BBC and has impressed those who have seen it. After some preliminaries, the documentary quoted a farmer as saying, "My family's been here for about four generations, since the late twenties, and we've had a field here about sixty years without seeing any circles at all." Then, pointing to a nearby crop circle, he explained why he knew it was a hoax:

> Because when you look at the center over there, you'll see that the ground has been trampled down much more than on the edge. I reckon if people linked arms and walked around in a circle, the person on the edge has traveled faster than the chap in the center, who's stood still. He's stood the corn [grain] down more in the center. You can clearly see this. Also I reckon they do this at nighttime because the people who do this don't want to be spotted because I'd be on their backs if they were caught.

He added:

> They've probably had a few pints . . . and they lurched, rather, into the corn because the line is not sharp; it's more like they staggered drunkenly out of line.[115]

At this point the BBC brought in "a young farmers' tug-of-war team," with the announcer sagely noting that "they looked surprisingly practiced as they made their way down the tracks left by the sprayers [i.e., down the tramlines] to the spot we'd chosen." Using a rope to establish a radius, they linked arms and in no time at all had produced what appeared to be a fine circle that one of them finished off by careful grooming on hands and knees. The announcer commented: "It was roughly at this point that serious doubts crept in and all sorts of little green men were replaced by images of large ruddy ones."

Challenged by the announcer's "Looks as if you'd done it before," the members of the team exchanged grins and knowing looks. Finally, one said, "Well, that would be telling. It's a trade secret. I wouldn't like to say. I think many farmers in Hampshire would be knocking on our doors."[116]

More recently, in September 1991, two "jovial con men in their sixties" claimed they had been responsible for many of the giant wheat-field patterns made over the years. In support of their claim, they fooled Delgado, who declared a pattern they had produced for the tabloid *Today* to be authentic; he said it was of a type no hoaxer could have made. The men said their equipment consisted of "two wooden boards, a piece of string and a bizarre sighting device attached to a baseball cap."[117] They demonstrated the technique for television crews—e.g., on ABC-TV's "Good Morning America," September 10, 1991—and their proclaimed hoax was publicized worldwide.

In the wake of such reports, *The Cereologist* commented in an editorial:

> The result of all this has been to throw the world of cereology into a state of total confusion. All its previous certainties have been demolished. Delgado has had to forfeit his pretensions to infallibility; Meaden has abandoned his plasma vortex theory as an explanation for pictograms; dowsers have been exposed as incapable of telling a genuine crop circle from a man-made one. Just as we predicted in a previous issue, Meaden has been betrayed and jettisoned by the authorities who previously made use of his theory as a cover-up explanation for the entire crop circle phenomenon. Both the Japanese

scientists and the provincial English ufologists who previously supported him have admitted that the hypothetical plasma vortex can not possibly be the cause of pictograms, and the common-sense belief, that the crop circle phenomenon is nothing but an elaborate hoax, is now established as the official doctrine.[118]

Indeed, a contest held in 1992, which cereologists thought would discredit the hoax hypothesis, proved otherwise: Several teams of crop-circle makers accepted the contest's restrictive, nighttime conditions and still produced a series of duplicate pictograms, including a prize-winning formation that was judged especially successful.[119]

The burden now remains with the die-hard cereologists to justify postulating anything other than hoaxes for the mystery circles. We feel their time would be better spent attempting to identify more of the hoaxers and to learn what motivates them to do their work. In a chapter titled "Theories Update" in his and Colin Andrews's *Crop Circles: The Latest Evidence,* Pat Delgado had promised cryptically, "What the energy is and who controls it will be explained at a time considered to be more fitting."[120] On the other hand, an insightful reviewer has characterized the circle effect as "a form of graffiti on the blank wall of southern England."[121]

Although the phenomenon has clearly exhibited aspects of social contagion like other fads and crazes—the goldfish-swallowing contest of 1939 comes to mind[122]—the graffiti analogy is especially apt. Just as graffiti is a largely clandestine activity produced by a variety of scribblers and sketchers possessed of tendencies to wreak mischief, urge religious fervor, provide social commentary, show off elaborate artistic skills, or the like, so the crop-circles phenomenon has seemingly tapped the varied motives of equally varied circle makers—from bored or mischievous farmhands, to UFO buffs and New Age mystics, to self-styled crop artists, and possibly others. The phenomenon is indeed mysterious, but the mystery may be only the ever-present one of human behavior.

Notes

1. See Pat Delgado and Colin Andrews, *Circular Evidence: A Detailed Investigation of the Flattened Swirled Crops Phenomenon* (Grand Rapids, Mich.: Phanes Press, 1989): see also George Terence Meaden, *The Circles Effect and Its Mystery* (Bradford-on-Avon, Wiltshire: Artetech, 1989), and "Field of Dreams," *Omni,* Dec. 1990, 62–67.

2. Meaden, *Circles Effect and Its Mystery;* Salley B. Donnelly, "Going Forever Around on Circles," *Time,* Sept. 11, 1989, 12.

3. Delgado and Andrews, *Circular Evidence,* 160–61.

4. "England Perplexed by Crop-field Rings," *Denver Post,* Oct. 29, 1989.

5. The tabloid *Today,* cited by Wendy Grossman, "Crop Circles Create Rounds of Confusion," *Skeptical Inquirer* 14, no. 2 (Winter 1990): 117.

6. BBC program "Country File," Oct. 9, 1988; Meaden, *Circles Effect and Its Mystery,* 87–88; Paul Fuller, "Mystery Circles: Myth in the Making," *International UFO Reporter,* May/June 1988: 5.

7. Meaden, *Circles Effect and Its Mystery,* 3, 11.

8. Ibid., 10–11, 57; Donnelly, "Going Forever Around in Circles," 12.

9. Meaden, *Circles Effect and Its Mystery,* 19, 60–66.

10. Fuller, "Mystery Circles," 8.

11. Meaden, *Circles Effect and Its Mystery,* 15.

12. Delgado and Andrews, *Circular Evidence,* 12–13.

13. Ibid., 60, 65, 74, 104.

14. Grossman, "Crop Circles Create Rounds of Confusion," 117.

15. Delgado and Andrews, *Circular Evidence,* 17, 63, 98.

16. Ibid., 189.

17. G. T. Meaden, "Crop Circles and the Plasma Vortex," in Ralph Noyes, ed., *The Crop Circle Enigma* (Bath, Eng.: Gateway Books, 1990), 82–83; Delgado and Andrews, *Circular Evidence,* 177; Grossman, "Crop Circles Create Rounds of Confusion," 118.

18. Meaden, *Circles Effect and Its Mystery,* 26–28; Jenny Randles and Paul Fuller, *Crop Circles: A Mystery Solved* (London: Robert Hale, 1990), 77.

19. Delgado and Andrews, *Circular Evidence,* 68.

20. Michael T. Shoemaker, "Measuring the Circles," *Strange Magazine* 6 (1990): 56.

21. "A Witness from Whitness," *Fortean Times* 53 (Winter 1989–90): 37.

22. For a bibliography of books, periodicals, articles, and other writings on the phenomenon, see Michael Chorost, "Circles of Note: A Continuing Bibliography," *MUFON UFO Journal* 276 (Apr. 1991): 14–17.

23. Quoted in Mike Sullivan, "MUFON's Circular Reasoning," *North Texas Skeptic* 5, no. 3 (May–June 1991): 1, 2.

24. See for example, Delgado and Andrews, *Circular Evidence,* 160–61, 165.

25. Ibid., "Worldwide Reports," 179–89; Ronald D. Story, *The Encyclopedia of UFOs* (Garden City, N.Y.: Doubleday, 1989), 370–71.

26. Gary Kinder, *Light Years: An Investigation into the Extraterrestrial Experience of Edward Meier* (New York: Atlantic Monthly Press, 1987), 15.

27. Meaden, *Circles Effect and Its Mystery,* 9.

28. Delgado and Andrews, *Circular Evidence,* 11–17.

29. Ralph Noyes, "Circular Arguments," *MUFON UFO Journal,* 258 (Oct. 1989): 18.

30. John Michell, "The Alien Corn," *The Spectator,* Aug. 12, 1989, 21.

31. Shoemaker, "Measuring the Circles," 56.

32. Michell, "Alien Corn," 21. (He does not review the Fuller and Randles book, *Crop Circles.*)

33. Ibid.

34. Dennis Pearce, report to Joe Nickell, July 21, 1991. (Pearce avoided the first, 1978 report, "because the details were so sketchy." He also noted that the reports for 1988 seemed incomplete, possibly as a result of the author's efforts to publish the book.)

35. G. Terence Meaden, "A Note on Observed Frequencies of Occurrence of Circles in British Cornfields," *Fortean Times* 53 (Winter 1989–90): 52–53.

36. Jenny Randles, "Nature's Crop Circles, Nature's UFOs," *International UFO Reporter,* May/June 1991, 14.

37. Meaden, "Note on Observed Frequencies," 53.

38. Noyes, *Crop Circle Enigma,* 49; Delgado and Andrews, *Circular Evidence,* 64.

39. "The Mowing Devil," *Fortean Times* 53 (Winter 1989–90): 38–39.

40. Shoemaker, "Measuring the Circles," 56.

41. Jenny Randles, "Measuring the Circles: Jenny Randles Responds," *Strange Magazine* 7 (April 1991): 26.

42. Pearce, op. cit.

43. Ibid.

44. Ibid., see also Randles and Fuller, *Crop Circles,* 21.

45. Donnelly, "Going Forever Around in Circles," 12.

46. "England Perplexed" (see n. 4).

47. Meaden, "Note on Observed Frequencies," 53.

48. Randles and Fuller, *Crop Circles,* 50.

49. Noyes, "Circular Arguments," 16.

50. Randles and Fuller, *Crop Circles,* 127 (fig. 7); Meaden, *Circles Effect and Its Mystery,* 106 (fig. 44).

51. John Michell, "Quarrels & Calamities of the Cereologists," *Fortean Times* 53 (Winter 1989–90): 42.

52. Randles and Fuller, *Crop Circles,* 22.

53. Fuller, "Mystery Circles," 6; Meaden, *Circles Effect and Its Mystery,* 37–45; Randles and Fuller, *Crop Circles,* 80.

54. Delgado and Andrews, *Circular Evidence,* 12, 167.

55. Some mystical cereologists imagine a correlation of circle sites with stone monuments, like Stonehenge, that they feel are laid out on so-called "ley lines." These are supposed to be anciently recognized "energy paths" that criss-cross the Earth and may be divined by dowsing rods and pendulums. However, Randles and Fuller state: "Paul Devereux, author of various books on the subject, editor of *The Ley Hunter* and widely considered the world's leading authority, told us flatly he sees no apparent connection. For us, that is that." ("Unsolved Mysteries," TV Program, Sept. 12, 1990; Randles and Fuller, *Crop Circles,* 59. See also Delgado and Andrews, *Circular Evidence,* 164–65, 178).

56. Pearce, op. cit.

57. Donna McGuire and Eric Adler, "More Puzzling Circles Found in Fields," (Kansas City, Mo.) *Star,* Sept. 21, 1990.

58. "Rings Mysteriously Appear in Wheat Fields," *Toronto Globe and Mail,* Sept. 25, 1990. The Japanese circles were reported on CNN "Headline News," Oct. 25, 1990.

59. Joe Nickell appeared by telephone on the "Andy Berry Show," CFRB Radio, Sept. 25, 1990.

60. Nick Martin, "Mysterious Circles in Fields Pose Cosmic Dilemma," *Winnipeg Free Press,* Oct. 21, 1990; "Crop Circles Profiled," *Tampa Bay Skeptics Report* 3.3 (Winter 1990–91): 6.

61. Delgado and Andrews, *Circular Evidence,* 17, 41–47, 95.

62. Ibid., 107. While this was new for the Wessex area, the formation is similar to some "discovered" by the Swiss contactee mentioned earlier; see n. 26.

63. Ibid., 122.

64. Ibid. 12.

65. This was on page 96 of the first (1989) edition of the book; the subsequent (1990) edition replaces "always" with "often."

66. Michell, "Quarrels and Calamities," 47.

67. Meaden, *Circles Effect and Its Mystery,* 9.

68. Randles, "Nature's Crop Circles," 14.

69. G. T. Meaden, "Crop Circles and the Plasma Vortex," in Noyes, *Crop Circle Enigma,* 76, 85.

70. Ibid., 85.

71. For color photographs, see Noyes, *Crop Circle Enigma,* 90–156, *passim;* "Field of Dreams" (see n. 1), 62–67.

72. "Mystery Circles in British Cornfields Throw a Curve to Puzzled Scientists," *Newark Star-Ledger,* Jan. 10, 1990.

73. "The Jillian Rice Show," KOA Denver, Aug. 19, 1990.

74. *Flying Saucer Review* 32, no. 6 (Nov. 1987), quoted in Randles and Fuller, *Crop Circles,* 18–19. See also "Circles," *The Skeptic* 10, no. 4 (Summer 1990): 14.

75. Randles, "Nature's Crop Circles," 14.

76. Ibid.

77. Delgado and Andrews, *Circular Evidence,* 126.

78. See plates 26 and 27 (with captions) in Noyes, *Crop Circle Enigma,* 91.

79. Delgado and Andrews, *Circular Evidence,* 74.

80. See plates 30 and 31 (with captions) in Noyes, *Crop Circle Enigma,* 93.

81. Delgado and Andrews, *Circular Evidence,* 155.

82. Ibid., 156.

83. Randles and Fuller, *Crop Circles,* 53.

84. Ibid.

85. Quoted in Delgado and Andrews, *Circular Evidence,* 25.

86. Noyes, *Crop Circle Enigma,* 28; Michell, "Quarrels and Calamities,"

47–48.

87. From a Reuters dispatch quoted in Larry F. Johnson, "Crop Circles," *The Georgia Skeptic* 4, no. 3 (May, June 1991): n.p.

88. Ibid.: "CBS News," July 25, 1990; Noyes, *Crop Circle Enigma,* 188; Associated Press report (e.g., in *The Buffalo News,* July 26, 1990). A somewhat similar series of events transpired in 1991, as reported in the July 27 *New York Times.*

89. Quoted in Randles and Fuller, *Crop Circles,* 29.

90. Noyes, *Crop Circle Enigma,* 30. (For photos see plates 25 and 26, page 91.)

91. Delgado and Andrews, *Circular Evidence,* 139.

92. Ibid., 51 (plates 22 and 23), 142 (plate 77; cf. Randles and Fuller, *Crop Circles,* fifth photo following page 64.)

93. Archie E. Roy, in the Foreword to Noyes, *Crop Circle Enigma,* 12.

94. Michell, "Quarrels and Calamities," 47.

95. Hilary Evans, "The Crop-circle Paradox," in Noyes, *Crop Circle Enigma,* 41.

96. Randles and Fuller, *Crop Circles,* 15.

97. Noyes, *Crop Circle Enigma,* 30.

98. The Earl of Haddington, letter to *The Cereologist* (Spring 1991), quoted in *The Skeptics UFO Newsletter* 10 (July 1991): 7.

99. Noyes, *Crop Circle Enigma,* 133; Lucy Pringle, "Headaches or Healing," in Noyes, *Crop Circle Enigma,* 182. For a skeptical discussion of dowsing see our *Secrets of the Supernatural* (Buffalo, N.Y.: Prometheus Books, 1983), 89–102.

100. John Michell, "What Mean These Marks?" in Noyes, *Crop Circle Enigma,* 45; Delgado and Andrews, *Circular Evidence,* 68.

101. Delgado and Andrews, *Circular Evidence,* 138.

102. Ibid., 51, 63–64.

103. Interviews by Joe Nickell with Dr. Morris J. Blitzer and Dr. Charles T. Daughtery, Agronomy Department, University of Kentucky, August 28, 1990.

104. Sullivan, "MUFON's Circular Reasoning," 1.

105. Ibid., 9. Minnesota skeptic Keith Pickering explains (in an unpublished monograph dated December 3, 1990): "The average person looking at a wheatfield sees a continuous blanket of grass. But this is just an illusion; in

reality, small grains are planted in rows just like corn. The difference is that the rows are typically 15 to 25 centimeters apart for small grains. This is not much room, but it is greater than the width of a human foot. So crossing a grainfield without leaving a track is really just like crossing a cornfield: you bend the plants out of the way, and you place your feet between the rows, not on them. Of course, greater care must be taken and the passage is slower; but the technique works." In addition, during the hours before the circle is discovered the plants may naturally spring back to their original position, "especially if there is a breeze during the night."

106. Randles and Fuller, *Crop Circles,* 72.

107. Dennis Stacy, "Hoaxes and a Whole Lot More," *MUFON UFO Journal* 277 (May 1991): 15.

108. Press reports, quoted in Randles and Fuller, *Crop Circles,* 97.

109.   Sullivan, "MUFON's Circular Reasoning," 3.

110. See Randles and Fuller, *Crop Circles,* 69.

111. Ibid., 64–65.

112. See, for example, Stacy, "Hoaxes and a Whole Lot More," 11.

113. In a July 1987 issue of *Southern Evening Echo* (Southhampton), quoted in Randles and Fuller, *Crop Circles,* 64.

114. Randles and Fuller, *Crop Circles,* 63–64.

115. "Country File" (see n. 6).

116. Ibid.

117. William E. Schmidt, "Two 'Jovial Con Men' Take Credit (?) for Crop Circles," *New York Times,* Sept. 10, 1991.

118. "Editorial Notes," *The Cereologist* 5 (Winter 1991–92): 2.

119. "Circle Hoax Contest," *Science* 257 (July 24, 1992): 481.

120. Pat Delgado and Colin Andrews, *Crop Circles: The Latest Evidence* (London: Bloomsbury, 1990).

121. Jerold R. Johnson, "Pretty Pictures," review of *Crop Circles: The Latest Evidence, MUFON UFO Journal* 275 (March 1991): 18.

122. Paul Sann, *Fads, Follies and Delusions of the American People* (New York: Bonanza Books, 1967), 289–92.

Select Bibliography

Chorost, Michael. "Circles of Note: A Continuing Bibliography." *MUFON UFO Journal* 276 (April 1991): 14–17.

Delgado, Pat, and Colin Andrews. *Circular Evidence: A Detailed Investigation of the Flattened Swirled Crops Phenomenon.* Grand Rapids, Mich.: Phanes Press, 1989. Profusely illustrated survey of circle patterns and details; unfortunately much given to mystery mongering.

Meaden, George Terence. *The Circles Effect and Its Mystery.* Bradford-on-Avon, Eng.: Artetech, 1989. Presentation of the "scientific" theory that crop circles are formed by "wind vortexes."

Noyes, Ralph, ed. *The Crop Circle Enigma.* Bath, Eng.: Gateway Books, 1990. A spectrum of views—from the sensible to the nonsensical—by various observers and cereologists; illustrated with color photos of elaborate crop circles and pictograms.

Randles, Jenny, and Paul Fuller. *Crop Circles: A Mystery Solved.* London: Robert Hale, 1990. Stubborn defense of a no-longer-defensible position (Meaden's wind-vortex theory), but with much valuable information nevertheless.

Acknowledgments

An abridged version of this chapter originally appeared as "The Crop-circle Phenomenon: An Investigative Report," *Skeptical Inquirer* 16, no. 2 (Winter 1992): 136–49.

We are grateful to the following persons for their help with this project: Dennis Pearce, for his computer analyses; Dr. Morris J. Blitzer and Dr. Charles T. Daughtery, for their professional opinions; Barry Karr, Lynda Harwood, and Kendrick Frazier of CSICOP for their research assistance and encouragement; J. Porter Henry, Jr., for transcribing the videotape of a BBC program; Joseph-Beth Booksellers, Lexington, Kentucky, for help in obtaining books. We also express our gratitude to the following, who provided assistance in various ways: Becky Long (Tucker, Georgia); Keith Pickering (Watertown, Minnesota); Dixon J. Wrapp (Sebastopol, California); Rob Aken (King Library, University of Kentucky, Lexington); Glenn Taylor, Robert H.

van Outer, and Dr. Robert A. Baker (Lexington, Kentucky); Janet and Doug Fetherling (Toronto, Canada); Christopher D. Allan (Stoke-on-Trent, England); Mr. and Mrs. Charles Hall (Southhampton, England); and to all others who have lent assistance, advice, and encouragement.

12

Afterword

Although we bring this casebook to a close, we are under no illusion that we have written the final word on all of the foregoing mysteries. While we have put forth what we believe is the most likely explanation in each case—the one predicated on the fewest assumptions, consistent with scholarly and scientific principles, and supported by corroborative evidence—we know that there will be those who remain unconvinced.

Among them may be those who intelligently and honestly reach a different conclusion. If they have better evidence, or can offer a more defensible hypothesis in a case, we certainly want to learn of it.

We do fear that some who disagree with us may simply be those who stubbornly embrace the mysterious, who prefer shadowy conspiracy theories or occult beliefs to more mundane realities. Such people will always find a pretext for keeping the fanciful alive, of course. Consider, for example, those who exaggerate the technical knowledge required of the Piltdown hoaxer (chap. 8) to look beyond the obvious culprit, Charles Dawson, for a more interesting suspect or a more intriguing motive.

Or, for another example, although Lee Harvey Oswald's body was exhumed, forensically identified, and laid to rest a second time (as related in chap. 3), scarcely had the last spadeful of earth been tamped on the grave than a tabloid asked, "When was Oswald's Body Switched?" Citing the opinions of a "top investigator"—one Mae Brussell, represented as president of something called World Watchers Incorporated— the paper announced: "Exhumation of JFK's assassin starts a whole new set of conspiracy theories." Brussell asserted, "Someone could have added the necessary dental proof so that the body would be consistent with Oswald's."[1]

Of course, the approach I took circumvents that particular argument—or at least it should—but one should never underestimated the perversity of conspiracy theorists. In any case, the larger questions raised by the Kennedy assassination will doubtless continue to elicit charge and countercharge. For example, the authors of a book titled *Death in Washington* claimed a former CIA agent served as the agency's case officer for Oswald and was linked to the killing of Kennedy and Chilean Foreign Minister Orlando Letelier. However, a legal action group that defends former U.S. intelligence officers forced a retraction of the claims in an out-of-court settlement, according to the *New York Times*.[2]

For yet another example of the persistence of belief, take Larry Arnold, the Pennsylvania schoolbus driver who continues to suggest (as we discussed in chap. 10) that Jack Angel experienced "spontaneous human combustion" (SHC), even though there is overwhelming evidence to the contrary. Neither Angel's own admission in legal proceedings that his burns resulted from scalding (caused by his releasing a safety valve on his motorhome's hot water heater), nor some fifteen points of corroborative evidence (the valve being discovered in the open position, Angel's burns having occurred without damaging his clothes, etc.), can dissuade Arnold.

For his part, Arnold says of the concept of SHC that he has "found it basically hopeless trying to convince the unbelievers." He adds: "As far as the scientific community goes, it's something they haven't come to terms with."[3]

But according to Jerome Clark, a former editor of *Fate* magazine who published Arnold's articles on SHC as well as ours:

> Not everything that claims to be a mystery is legitimate, and I just don't believe the evidence is there. Larry has done a lot more on this than anyone I know of, but he goes into this with a pro-mystical point of view seeking to have his point of view validated.[4]

To take one more example, there is Stanton T. Friedman's response to the proof that the "MJ-12" crashed-saucer papers are forgeries (as demonstrated in chap. 6). When it was shown that the Truman signature on one document was identical to one on a genuine Truman letter, thus clearly demonstrating that the questioned document was an amateurish paste-up-type of forgery, Friedman refused to accept the proof. He claimed the signatures were "not identical at all"[5] because one would not precisely superimpose over the other—a fact that document experts knew was simply due to minor stretching caused by photocopying.

Wading into the dispute was Ted R. Spickler, Ph.D., who demonstrated that, when the signature on the MJ-12 document was shrunk by 3 percent, it superimposed precisely over the authentic signature.[6] Whether Friedman will accept this proof is doubtful. In his *Final Report on Operation Majestic 12,* he fails even to mention our report on the forgery.[7]

In contrast, the Center for UFO Studies, in an anthology titled *The Roswell Report: A Historical Perspective,* republished our report, followed by a supportive article by Don Schmitt and Kevin D. Randle. In their "The MJ-12 Document: A Hoax," Schmitt and Randle find our analysis "devastating" and offer much supportive evidence. For example, they say of the MJ-12 briefing paper for President-elect Eisenhower:

> On page three of the briefing paper there is a paragraph that explains that a rancher in New Mexico reported the crash "northwest of Roswell Army Air Base (now Walker Field)." Both references to

the base at Roswell are wrong. It was Roswell Army Air Field and then Walker Air Force Base. (It is interesting to note that similar mistakes about the names of military bases are consistently made by Jaime Shandera and Bill Moore. *The Roswell Incident* refers to the base at Roswell as the Roswell Army Air Base throughout the book. In a *Focus* editorial, "Enough is Too Much," Moore writes about the Fort Worth Army Air Base.)[8]

With some of our investigations, new evidence may yet be discovered that will add further corroboration to the solution we have offered or will warrant reexamination of the case, whether by us or by other investigators. Or the new material may be hilariously irrelevant, like that in an article on crop circles (the subject of chap. 11) that appeared in a fringe magazine titled *The Journal of Borderland Research*. Carrying the byline Searlas Eadbhard, the article purports to "demonstrate scientifically the principles of language" found in the crop circles.[9]

The claim is that "the circles, arcs, rings, spurs, forks and rectangles" of the crop designs "are indeed alphabet letters." After the shapes are analyzed, "The findings are then projected by syllables/words into the Gaelic and then translated into English." An example is given of a set of concentric circles reported in 1990. The central circle was of standing grain, the next of burnt stubble, the outer of flattened grain "with no directional information." Translated, it supposedly reads: "Immersion great it is. Out of It is a voice; alas of man evil in, of life with, whence a torch from, a punishment from a younger wanderer."[10] Now could someone please translate the translation? The writer does concede that the translation represents only "ONE possible permutation."[11]

We wait to hear further on these or some of our other cases. In the meantime, we are already at work on new investigations, already venturing into yet additional "mysterious realms."

Notes

1. Chris Forsyth, "When Was Oswald's Body Switched?" *Globe,* Oct. 27, 1981.

2. "Ex-C.I.A. Agent Gains Retraction by Authors," *New York Times,* Feb. 16, 1986.

3. Gary Rotstein, "Burning Issue: Can Body Consume Itself in a Flash Burst of Heat?" *Post-Gazette* (Pennsylvania), Nov. 28, 1985.

4. Ibid.

5. Stanton T. Friedman, "MJ-12: The Jury is Still Out," *International UFO Reporter,* March/April 1990, 14.

6. Ted R. Spickler, "The Truman MJ-12 Letter," *International UFO Reporter,* May/June 1991, 12–13.

7. Stanton Friedman, *Final Report on Operation Majestic 12* (Mt Ranier, Md.: Fund for UFO Research, 1990).

8. Don Schmitt and Kevin D. Randle, "The MJ-12 Document: A Hoax," in George M. Eberhard, ed., *The Roswell Report: A Historical Perspective* (Chicago: Center for UFO Studies, 1991), 131.

9. Searlas Eadbhard, "The Word on Crop Circles," *Journal of Borderland Research* 47, no. 4 (July–August 1991): 18.

10. Ibid., 18, 20.

11. Ibid., 20.

Index